ROLE REVERSAL

Achieving Uncommonly Excellent Results in the Student-Centered Classroom

mark
barnes

ASCD

Alexandria, Virginia USA

1703 N. Beauregard St. • Alexandria, VA 22311-1714 USA
Phone: 800-933-2723 or 703-578-9600 • Fax: 703-575-5400
Web site: www.ascd.org • E-mail: member@ascd.org
Author guidelines: www.ascd.org/write

Gene R. Carter, *Executive Director;* Mary Catherine (MC) Desrosiers, *Chief Program Development Officer;* Richard Papale, *Publisher;* Laura Lawson, *Acquisitions Editor;* Julie Houtz, *Director, Book Editing & Production;* Jamie Greene, *Editor;* Lindsey Smith, *Graphic Designer;* Mike Kalyan, *Production Manager;* Keith Demmons, *Desktop Publishing Specialist*

© 2013 by ASCD. All rights reserved. No part of this publication may be reproduced or transmitted in any form or by any means, electronic or mechanical, including photocopy, recording, or any information storage and retrieval system, without permission from ASCD. Readers who wish to duplicate material copyrighted by ASCD may do so for a small fee by contacting the Copyright Clearance Center (CCC), 222 Rosewood Dr., Danvers, MA 01923, USA (phone: 978-750-8400; fax: 978-646-8600; Web: www.copyright.com). For requests to reprint rather than photocopy, contact ASCD's permissions office: 703-575-5749 or permissions@ascd.org. Translation inquiries: translations@ascd.org.

Printed in the United States of America. Cover art © 2013 by ASCD. ASCD publications present a variety of viewpoints. The views expressed or implied in this book should not be interpreted as official positions of the Association.

All Web links in this book are correct as of the publication date below but may have become inactive or otherwise modified since that time. If you notice a deactivated or changed link, please e-mail books@ascd.org with the words "Link Update" in the subject line. In your message, please specify the Web link, the book title, and the page number on which the link appears.

ASCD Member Book, No. FY13-5 (Feb. 2013, P). ASCD Member Books mail to Premium (P), Select (S), and Institutional Plus (I+) members on this schedule: Jan., PSI+; Feb., P; Apr., PSI+; May, P; July, PSI+; Aug., P; Sept., PSI+; Nov., PSI+; Dec., P. Select membership was formerly known as Comprehensive membership.

PAPERBACK ISBN: 978-1-4166-1506-4   ASCD product #113004

Also available as an e-book (see Books in Print for the ISBNs).

Quantity discounts for the paperback edition only: 10–49 copies, 10%; 50+ copies, 15%; for 1,000 or more copies, call 800-933-2723, ext. 5634, or 703-575-5634. For desk copies: member@ascd.org.

Library of Congress Cataloging-in-Publication Data

Barnes, Mark.
    Role reversal : achieving uncommonly excellent results in the student-centered class-room / Mark Barnes.
        pages cm
    Includes bibliographical references and index.
    ISBN 978-1-4166-1506-4 (pbk. : alk. paper) 1. Classroom management–United States. 2. Teaching–United States. 3. Teacher-student relationships–United States. 4. Educational tests and measurements–United States. I. Title.
    LB3013.B32 2013
    371.117–dc23
                            2012041723

21 20 19 18 17 16 15 14 13   1 2 3 4 5 6 7 8 9 10 11 12

For my children, Ethan and Lauren,
who inspire me to attempt to make education better.

Imagine a school system that recognizes learning is natural, that a love of learning is normal, and that real learning is passionate learning. A school curriculum that values questions above answers . . . creativity above fact regurgitation . . . individuality above conformity . . . and excellence above standardized performance. . . . And we must reject all notions of 'reform' that serve up more of the same: more testing, more 'standards,' more uniformity, more conformity, more bureaucracy.

—Tom Peters, *Re-Imagine*

ROLE REVERSAL

Achieving Uncommonly
Excellent Results in the
Student-Centered Classroom

Referenced Products

·······························

About.com® is a registered trademark of About.com, Inc.

Animoto® is a registered trademark of Animoto, Inc.

Best Buy® is a registered trademark of BBY Solutions, Inc

Diigo.com™ is a trademark of Diigo, Inc.

Edmodo® is a registered trademark of Edmodo, Inc.

Evernote® is a registered trademark of Evernote Corporation.

Facebook® is a registered trademark of Facebook, Inc.

Fact Monster® is a registered trademark of Pearson Education, Inc.

Glogster® is a registered trademark of Glogster, A.S.

Goodreads® is a registered trademark of Goodreads, Inc.

Google® and YouTube® are trademarks of Google, Inc.

iPad®, iPhone®, and iPod® are registered trademarks of Apple, Inc.

Jing® is a registered trademark of TechSmith Corporation.

KidBlog® is a registered trademark of Kidblog Inc.

Kindle® is a registered trademark of Amazon.com, Inc.

Noodle Tools® is a registered trademark of NoodleTools, Inc.

Nook® is a registered trademark of Barnes & Noble, Inc.

ProBoards® is a registered trademark of ProBoards, Inc.

Skype™ is a trademark of Skype.

Twitter® is a registered trademark of Twitter, Inc.

Ujam® is a registered trademark of UJAM, Inc.

Voki® is a registered trademark of Oddcast, Inc.

Wikipedia® is a registered trademark of Wikipedia Foundation, Inc.

All other referenced marks are the property of their respective owners.

Acknowledgments

I'd like to thank several special colleagues who have been inspirational to me during my work in creating a Results Only Learning Environment: John Richards, Riley Parke, Ron Petrecca, Lisa Hubler, Chrissy Pease, John Romanoff, Paula Morgan, Supriya Culliton, Barry Hartz, Laurie Ayers-Hughey, Dottie LeBlanc, Lori Sandel, Ron Johnson, Elaine Schwartz, Brett Spicer, Dave DeWitt, Donna Levy, Marc Caruso, Deb Long, Jeff Adick, Brian Bruce, Christine Creviston, and Stefani Slain. Whether you realize it or not, at some point, we've had discussions that helped me think this through and make it a reality. Thanks for listening and for your ongoing feedback.

Thanks to the wonderful students who wrote introductions to numerous chapters. They beautifully represent the Results Only Learning Environment's most important stakeholders.

Thanks to the fine educators who are quoted in the book and took the time to answer personal inquiries about their methods. I truly value their time and input.

Thanks to the entire ASCD team for its kindness and dedication. I want to extend my deepest gratitude to ASCD's Laura Lawson. Without her unparalleled professionalism, vision, and constant encouragement, this project would have died before it ever got started. Thanks to ASCD editor Jamie Greene, whose tireless efforts and thoughtful insights make my words a little less cumbersome.

Thanks Mom and Dad for teaching me to be a good husband, father, and dedicated public servant and for giving me so much. I love you both.

Thank you Mollie for being my most valued critic and sounding board. Without your unwavering support, I would be lost. I love you more every day.

Introduction

Sasha was off to a rough start in her 7th grade year. During the first grading period, she did very little school work. She completed a small part of one major language arts project and did nothing on a second. When she was asked to review material covered on a web-based assessment, so she could retake it and improve her poor score, Sasha did not produce once again. In-class activities were done haphazardly, with little attention to detail. Feedback from her teacher—me—was mostly ignored.

At the end of the grading period, it was time for reflection, self-evaluation, and a final grade. I met with Sasha, as I did with every student, and we discussed her production. When I asked her for her thoughts, she admitted that the results were not what she had hoped for. She gave no excuses. Because the administration at the middle school where I teach mandates that teachers assign quarterly grades, I told Sasha that a formal grade had to go on her report card. This was a fairly new concept for her because there had been no points, percentages, or grades on any activity for the first nine weeks of school in our class.

"Put a grade on your production for Quarter One," I said. Tears rolled down Sasha's face, which was a heart-wrenching sight as I hated to see her punished by a grade. Between sobs, her chin resting weakly on her chest, Sasha whispered, "I guess it has to be an *F*." When I asked if she was certain, Sasha nodded affirmatively. It was at this very moment that I realized that a Results Only Learning Environment (ROLE) would forever change how I teach and how my students learn. One grading period later, Sasha was up to a *C*, and she continued to progress throughout the year. The roles were reversing. My students were taking control of their own learning and their own assessment. Education was becoming something truly revolutionary.

My Way or the Highway

Until just a few years ago, I was the kind of teacher whom I hated when I was a student—a my-way-or-the-highway kind of guy. I was brought up to believe that the teacher is always right, no matter how wrong he or she actually may be. "Just keep quiet, and do what you're told," my parents always said. I bought in to this because I knew there would be serious repercussions at home if I did not. I suppose it helped; I stayed out of trouble and made average grades, which kept both of my working parents satisfied. When I became a teacher, which is its own ironic story, I adopted my parents' theory: students should sit at their desks, remain quiet, always raise their hands, and do what they're told. I even relished reminding them of this at the beginning of each year.

"It's my way or the highway," I would announce on day one. "Do as I tell you and we'll get along fine. You might even learn a thing or two by the end of the school year." Of course, the 12-year-olds lined up in front of me just rolled their eyes and pretty much tolerated me year after year. Like most new teachers, I believed I had a lot of fresh ideas that would change education. For the most part, though, I was simply regurgitating information the same way my predecessors had for decades. My students' days consisted of standard rules and consequences, worksheets, bell work, homework, and multiple-choice tests, many of which I had borrowed from teachers who had been using them for 20 years or more. I lasted seven years teaching this way, and then I left education for the laudable profession of mortgage lending. That move lasted one year before I returned to the classroom—mainly because my wife is also a teacher, and I missed being able to share breaks together. After four more boring years of droning at students about classroom rules and the fundamentals of writing, I realized it was time for another change—in the classroom.

The Dawn of Technology

Because my students enjoyed the Internet, I decided to integrate as much of it as I could into my teaching. This began the transformation that this book is really about. Students wanted more technology, so I learned as much about Web 2.0 and social media as I could and started experimenting with methods of incorporating these applications into weekly or even daily lessons. A new enthusiasm for learning among my students made me realize that the old my-way-or-the-highway approach to teaching simply didn't work. Students knew what they wanted, so I started giving it to them. Suddenly, teaching became teaching *and* learning—and it was fun. I loved using technology so much that I created numerous professional development courses for educators. I could teach them how to replicate the success I was having. I was teaching at school and at home, and I finally felt like I was making the kind of contribution that I'd dreamed of making when I first became a teacher.

Then something awful happened, and the thrill of my new methods ended as suddenly as it began. Another school year, my 16th as a teacher, brought a new group of 7th graders, most of whom had little interest in web-based learning. Many had no interest in learning at all. In fact, this particular group had been labeled year after year by teachers in my district as "the bad bunch." This class was lowering district test scores and making principals and teachers think about early retirement.

"Just keep them busy, and try to survive the year," I was told by several colleagues who had encountered these students in prior school years. I listened, followed their instructions, and had my worst year ever as an educator. These students were greeted by the old Mr. Barnes—the one I thought had disappeared. For five periods a day, five days a week, and 180 school days, I showered them with worksheets and independent work.

"They aren't mature enough to work cooperatively," I told a colleague. "They'll just waste the whole period being disruptive." Dinner conversations that year often began with "I had a decent day; I only sent two kids to the principal's office." I faced each morning with dread, knowing I'd do very little, if any, real teaching. I survived that year, knowing that if I didn't reinvent myself, I'd have to leave the teaching profession—for good this time.

That summer brought a much-needed vacation that turned out to include far more than spending time with my family and perfecting my golf swing. Although I'm not typically someone who searches the self-help aisle in book stores or libraries, I felt the need for something inspirational. I purchased Daniel Pink's book *Drive: The Surprising Truth about What Motivates Us* the summer after dealing with "the bad bunch." From page one, I was intrigued. After a few chapters and examples of Pink's research, I was captivated. Although I'm not here to endorse Pink's book or any of the others that I'll reference, I will say that the concepts in *Drive* were truly life-altering for me, and I'd recommend the book to anyone, especially teachers. In the past decade, I had suffered through many professional development sessions that offered nothing truly enlightening. This time, though, my enthusiasm was not based on a false hope acquired from a random Ph.D. spouting irrelevancies in a half-day workshop on assertive discipline. The summer after "the bad bunch" was different. I devoured Pink's work, along with books by as many of the people he had researched as I could. I carefully reviewed a business model, created by former Best Buy executives Cali Ressler and Jody Thompson, called the Results-Only Work Environment, and I considered how this system might function in my own classroom. I read Alfie Kohn's *The Homework Myth* and *Beyond Discipline* and Donalyn Miller's *The Book Whisperer*. Articles by Steven Krashen on successful reading strategies for K–12 teachers often lit up my computer screen. Each of these managers, researchers, consultants, and educators reshaped my view of teaching in general and effective methods of instruction in particular.

I reevaluated my 16 years as a classroom teacher and gave special consideration to rapport building, cooperative learning, assessment, and classroom management. I asked myself plenty of questions. What had worked with my students? What didn't work? Why was the previous year such a monumental failure for a veteran teacher who had seen almost everything? Most important, how could things have been different, and how might I apply the concepts I'd recently studied to my own teaching? Could I reinvent my classroom? How could I truly impact my students? What exactly would turn even the most reluctant learners into hard-working, knowledge-thirsty young adults? Could I change from a traditional teacher into something completely different?

Change That Changes Everything

Change can be frightening. At the same time, it can also be exhilarating or even life-altering. A simple change can touch a single person, or it can affect thousands—even millions—of people. A few years ago, the changes I made in my approach to teaching altered my life and the lives of my students. With equal parts trepidation and excitement, I transformed my classroom into what I call a Results Only Learning Environment—a fascinating place where students willingly strive to learn. It wasn't easy; changing how I taught meant admitting that something was wrong. This is a difficult thing for most people to face, but I

A | Thumbnail View of a Results Only Learning Environment (ROLE)

Workshop Setting Is the Norm

In a ROLE, students collaborate daily, and various activities take place at the same time. Here are the elements of a results-only learning workshop:

- Desks are in pods.
- Creature comforts exist: area rugs, beanbag chairs, magazine racks, etc.
- Electronic devices (used for mobile learning) are welcome.
- There is a quiet chaos—movement, talking, sharing.

Coach/Facilitator Replaces Teacher

A student-centered, collaborative learning community does not need a sage-on-the-stage traditional teacher. The ROLE teacher

- Delivers brief, interactive lessons (3–5 minutes).
- Understands how to integrate technology into learning.
- Creates year-long projects that encompass a wide array of learning outcomes.
- Delivers meaningful narrative feedback on all activities.
- Builds rapport with all students.

Traditional Methods Do Not Exist

The following methods are eliminated:

- Worksheets
- Homework
- Tests and quizzes
- Lectures
- Grades

Feedback Replaces Number and Letter Grades

Detailed narrative feedback, using the SE2R system (Summarize, Explain, Redirect, Resubmit), eliminates the need for punitive points, percentages, and letter grades.

Rules and Consequences Disappear

ROLE students manage themselves, so there is no need for old-style classroom management.

think it's even tougher for educators, since we seem to be wired a bit differently than other professionals. Teachers often make the worst students. We spend so much time advancing our degrees and developing professionally that it's easy to fall prey to the false belief that everything we do is right. Anyone who knows me personally would likely say that I have always been abundantly confident in my work. I was someone who liked to believe that what he was doing was right. The problem was that my confidence wasn't always built on research. If I saw even a modicum of success in something I tried in class, I believed it was the correct way to teach. When things went wrong, I blamed my students or their parents. I functioned this way for 16 years, before that one remarkable summer and the subsequent school year when I turned my classroom into a ROLE. Now, with the publication of this book, I hope that every teacher who reads it will also change, and a reform movement might begin.

A ROLE Up Close

To get the most out of this book, you have to consider the possibility of making your own dramatic changes—no matter what grade or subject you teach. Results-only learning is a system that eliminates most methods teachers currently use. It involves embracing the final result of learning rather than focusing on traditional practices, such as homework, worksheets, tests, and grades. A Results Only Learning Environment looks different from most classrooms (see Figure A). A ROLE classroom is characterized by

- A bustle that is often perceived inaccurately as mayhem by the casual observer.
- An absence of rules and consequences.
- Students who move about freely and congregate in small groups.
- Students who talk often.

- Different groups of students that simultaneously work independently and collaborate quietly.

Students in a ROLE decide how to demonstrate mastery of learning outcomes without being constrained by standards and pedagogy. Results-only learning hinges on formative assessment, primarily through ongoing, meaningful narrative feedback. Gone are number and letter grades; they are replaced with specific verbal and written feedback that carefully tells students how to make effective changes to activities and projects. A ROLE provides year-long projects, which empower students to build on the skills they learn, honing and expanding them as the school year passes.

For teachers whose school districts live and die by standardized testing, ROLE strategies address standards in a way that students learn them almost without realizing what they've done. Because of this, teaching to a standardized test becomes unnecessary. Students master learning outcomes in an enjoyable, project-based workshop setting that challenges them with real-world learning scenarios. A ROLE eliminates inert knowledge—material that students memorize for quizzes and tests but never remember later in life (Perkins, 2008). When faced with a high-stakes test, I've found that students who have spent the school year in a ROLE, learning things they can connect to the real world, typically outperform their peers in traditional classes who have spent most of their nine months in school focused on rote memorization and disconnected activities.

The individual parts of a Results Only Learning Environment are not revolutionary. Many teachers use cooperative learning, and many have done away with "old-school" rules and consequences. Project-based and inquiry learning have become popular models in plenty of school districts. A few teachers have even done away with traditional grading. So how is results-only learning unique? The answer is that a ROLE is greater than the sum of its parts. Results-only learning combines all of the aforementioned strategies, creating one remarkable community of learners who develop a genuine thirst for knowledge. Students in a ROLE collaborate willingly because they choose their own groups. They discuss openly because they are not inhibited by a traditional worksheet or assignment that bores them with repetition and rote memorization. They work outside of class, knowing that they decide what to do and when to complete it. They realize they'll never be punished by a 0 or an *F* if they don't complete a class activity on a given night. They enjoy class and like the teacher because he or she does not try to control them. Students go to the bathroom when they need to and return to their lockers to retrieve items without being admonished for doing so; the teacher provides an almost surreal kind of freedom.

Most important, ROLE students thrive on narrative feedback. They complete activities, knowing their teacher will not evaluate their hard work by placing a number or a letter on it. If something is not done right, the ROLE student will be told specifically what was missed and what still needs to be done. In order to demonstrate mastery learning, the student is directed back to a previous lesson or presentation and given an opportunity to make changes or additions to the current activity or assignment. Students know that missing a due date while perfecting a project is not a problem because results-only learning is stress-free, as all learning should be.

I recognize that the isolated parts of a Results Only Learning Environment—autonomy, collaboration, elimination of rules and consequences, narrative feedback, and project-based learning—may not be new to you. The marriage of these progressive methods, however, creates a system that is both unique and amazing. It is an environment that will free you from the bonds of traditional teaching. Imagine how enjoyable your job would be if the endless grading of homework and worksheets were eliminated. Consider the amount of stress that would be alleviated if you established an excellent rapport with students and parents. What if you never again had a discipline issue in your class? This book will show you all of this in action. It will guide you through results-only learning strategies and clearly demonstrate how to transform your classroom into a bustling community of learners who thirst for knowledge for the sake of acquiring it, rather than for a grade. This transformative approach to teaching is based on the research, theory, and practice of many remarkable educators and writers. Proof of the effectiveness of results-only learning, though, is based on my own practical experience and that of others who use ROLE strategies in their classrooms. As results-only learning is defined and explained, you'll meet numerous practitioners from across the United States and Canada, each with his or her own unique examples of in-class success stories. Most telling, though, are the astonishing achievements of ROLE students and the stories they share. Throughout the book, students' observations and anecdotes clarify what results-only learning looks like from the point of view of its most treasured stakeholders.

When you are finished reading, I believe you will have the same epiphany I had years ago, when I moved to a Results Only Learning Environment—teaching and learning should look different now from how it has looked during the past few decades. If you are willing to consider something new, something truly transformational, it just might be the life-altering change you've been waiting for.

Rebelling Against
Traditional Methods

Learning is always rebellion. . . . Every bit of new truth discovered is revolutionary to what was believed before.

—*Margaret Lee Runbeck*

As someone who has been both a teacher-in-training and a cooperative teacher, I have found that educators are taught from their preservice days that control is essential for success in the K–12 classroom. Perhaps, if we were to rethink this lone aspect of preparing young teachers, education would be immediately and markedly improved. Since virtually every education professor and cooperating teacher in the United States focuses on teaching young educators to be efficient classroom managers, this isn't likely to change anytime soon. This is unfortunate, because letting go of as much control as possible may be the single most important part of creating a successful classroom.

When I decided to take a risk and completely change my classroom into a Results Only Learning Environment, I knew the first thing I'd have to do is eliminate control. By evaluating the disaster that was the year of "the bad bunch," I quickly realized that what I had been taught as a preservice teacher and what I had practiced for so long were in direct conflict with what I wanted to achieve. People are motivated by three things: autonomy, mastery, and purpose (Pink, 2009). In the K–12 classroom, autonomy rarely exists; it definitely cannot thrive in the controlled world that most teachers believe is crucial to their success. In order to create a results-only classroom, I set out to replace control with autonomy on the first day of school.

Any skilled teacher will admit that the first day of school is critical to the success of the entire year. Not only is a first impression made, but expectations and rules are defined. Students learn if the classroom will be characterized by order or chaos. In the past, my "day one" consisted of an introduction, which was followed by this tired refrain: "Here's what we'll do this year. . . . These are my expectations. . . . Here are the rules. . . ." Oh, and let's not forget the ever-popular "It's my way or the highway." This was greeted by rolling eyes, heavy sighs, and groans of "Do we really have to read that?" or "Umm, I read that in 5th grade." Of course, my response to the latter was always, "Great! Then you should be my expert." (Just what 13-year-olds need—a smart alec for a role model.) This, of course, was prior to that amazing summer of research and change—before I discovered and devoured the work of Daniel Pink, Alfie Kohn, and Donalyn Miller.

Introducing the ROLE to Students

My first day of school now begins with far more than an introduction and a list of boring expectations. After all, in a results-only classroom, everything needs to be more about the students and less about the teacher. Although I'm convinced it's unintentional, it is true that many teachers tend to be a bit self-centered. However, a results-only classroom runs best when the teacher is hardly noticed by the casual observer. Therefore, on that first day, after I introduce myself, I begin explaining how the classroom functions.

"Welcome to our Results Only Learning Environment," I say. "Let me begin by telling you that this class will be different from any you've ever had." *Sure, it will*, they think; I can see it on their faces. I get their attention, though, with the following list of questions:

1. "Who in here loves homework?" No one.
2. "Who likes taking notes from a textbook?" Again, no hands.
3. "Who would love to have lots of tests and quizzes?" A chorus of groans.
4. "Who likes a lot of classroom rules?" Even more groans.
5. "Who enjoys being told what to do all the time?" They are 13 years old; the response is obvious.

"Isn't this what school is about, though?" I ask. They nod (on day one, kids have very little to say, as they're still feeling us out). "Not in this classroom," I announce. "Let me to show you how things are really different in here." At this point, I share a brief presentation that explains the fundamentals of the results-only classroom. The slides, as you may have guessed, include statements that are in direct contrast to the questions I just asked. The presentation begins.

In our Results Only Learning Environment

1. There is no homework.
2. There is no copying of anything from a textbook or whiteboard.
3. There are no tests or quizzes.
4. There are no classroom rules.
5. Students choose much of what they learn and how they learn it.

At first, there's silence. I give students time to absorb this completely unexpected information, before I ask them what they think. Although some raise their hands, this is where there is plenty of shouting out. "No rules?" "Seriously, you don't assign homework?" "No rules?" "So, I don't have to copy notes? Do I need a notebook?" "You really don't assign any homework?"

Once calm is restored, I explain. "Although I realize most teachers assign homework, my feeling is that homework is not necessary in order for you to demonstrate learning." At this point, there are plenty of furrowed eyebrows, and the whispers begin. "Tests and quizzes are a poor way to evaluate what you know. Too many of the questions are multiple choice, which doesn't tell me if you really know the answer. You will be able to show me what you know in your own way." I explain that this is a project-based class with plenty of time devoted to the completion of work. Students will have a variety of choices on all projects, so they can demonstrate learning the best way they know how. Of course, this is all demonstrated in a web-based presentation with plenty of engaging pictures, graphics, audio, and video and as little from me as possible.

"What about rules?" They can't get this one off their minds. I invite students to look around the room, and I ask, "How many Dos and Don'ts do you see posted?" They see nothing of the kind, because I have none; in fact, my room is quite bare on day one. Since a results-only class is student-centered, I rely on my students to produce most of what goes on the walls. I don't waste time posting rules or asking students to read rules that are unnecessary in a ROLE.

Classroom Make-up Doesn't Matter

While you imagine the potential chaos in a classroom without rules or assume that I have perfect students who never misbehave, let me be clear about a few things. I have a diverse group of 100–120 students each year. In a given school year, roughly 60 percent of my students are minorities, and 10–15 percent have Individualized Education Programs (IEPs). About one-third of my students qualify for our free-and-reduced-lunch program. I have students with learning disabilities, students with ADHD, emotionally disturbed students, and students with autism. In spite of this remarkable diversity, I rarely have discipline issues, and I almost never send students to a principal for disciplinary action.

This may be hard to believe, and it definitely wasn't always the case. Back in the my-way-or-the-highway days, I constantly sent students

to either our student management room (a euphemism for the detention area) or to the principal in charge of discipline. Remember those
all-too-regular dinner conversations when I considered two dismissed
students to be a good day? Those conversations are over. Later in this
book, I outline simple measures you can take to enjoy the same success with student behavior that I have found in a results-only system.
Before you jump ahead, though, take special note of the other parts of
a ROLE. It will become apparent that there's not one simple formula to
eliminate classroom management issues. Success is not based on an
assertive discipline, extrinsic rewards, or a step-by-step program. It is
the results-only system that creates a learning environment free from
behavior problems.

Let me emphasize here that I steer clear of posted rules and begin
the school year talking about mutual respect. This may sound trite, but
as we continue, the effectiveness of this system will become transpar-
ent. It's more involved than simply announcing on day one that we must
respect one another. If I want my students to embrace this approach,
then it is critical that I gain their respect on the first day of school.
That respect begins with a mutual faith in the Results Only Learning
Environment—terminology that is completely foreign to my students
in August—which is grounded in a simple list of assertions I make on
day one, along with an explanation for how the system affects us all.

Become a Rebel

Remember, I tell my students that we have no homework, no tests,
and no rules. More important, I declare that they will be given autonomy.
Since they have never known much freedom in the classroom, students immediately see me as a rebel—something that ignites a unique
curiosity and excitement in them. As odd and perhaps illogical as this
may seem, respect is created immediately because I'm discarding all
the procedures that students have been preconditioned to believe

are fundamental to every classroom—the very procedures they have grown to detest. Trust hasn't been built yet, but the simple notion that I'm breaking the rules earns me respect, or at least cooperation. This is an enormous accomplishment; when students like and respect you, no matter what the reason may be, they are more inclined to behave appropriately. Most teachers believe that when students are disrespectful, they simply haven't been taught respect at home. In some cases, this is probably true. In my experience, though, no matter how little they may have been taught about respect, even students whom other teachers typically consider disrespectful are cooperative in a Results Only Learning Environment—at least initially because of the rebel approach. There will be a fundamental shift in this attitude, as the year progresses, when students grow to respect the ROLE teacher not just as a rebel teacher but also as the facilitator of a learning system they grow to love. The vision of the rebel will fade, but the respect will remain. The important premise here is that, regardless of whether it's called respect or cooperation, the results-only classroom runs efficiently with little disruption from students.

To underscore the effectiveness of this rebel approach, consider the presentations students typically see on the first day of class. Most teachers begin with introductions, expectations, rules, required texts, and maybe a syllabus. Some even send a letter home to parents, outlining these things. After the first day of my class, most students leave shaking their heads, thinking I'm either very cool or very crazy. Either way, the majority leave liking me. I used to say that it was unimportant if students liked me. They could even believe I was mean, I'd boast to colleagues; I only wanted their respect and their learning. Ironically, I was getting neither. Although it may not be the most important part of teaching, getting students to like you is inherently linked to procuring their cooperation, respect, and learning (Montalvo, Mansfield, & Miller, 2007). Stand in front of them on day one and list the rules and they may not hate you, but they won't immediately like you, either. You may not be the coolest teacher around (I'm certainly not), but take a moment to ask yourself if students think, at the very least, that you're likable. There's plenty of research that says students perform better when they have positive relationships with their teachers (e.g., Marzano & Marzano, 2003; Schaps, 2003; Sullo, 2009), but my own experience is what convinced me. In the my-way-or-the-highway days, students were disruptive and accomplished very little. In the results-only classroom, there are virtually no disruptions and students complete almost every activity I assign.

What Do You Mean There Are No Grades?

Students get more excited when I explain the results-only system and tell them how teaching and assessment work. It's essential that they understand what project-based learning means, so I share some of the first project guidelines with them as models. The summer reading project, which is used to evaluate basic comprehension, writing, and creativity, is set up like a menu with appetizers, entrees, and desserts. Each part of the "meal" contains a variety of choices. This is where autonomy plays such a huge role. Students, just like everyone else, need to be given freedom; they are "meant to be autonomous individuals, not individual automatons" (Pink, 2009, p. 106). Since most of my students don't understand this, explaining autonomy and the choice that accompanies it is important, as is connecting it back to our initial project.

There is usually one student who asks how many points our first project is worth, which I love. If they don't ask, then I pose the question to them. "So, what do you think a project of this magnitude is worth?" Most of them are still thinking about points and grades, so I really shock them when I explain that there are never any points in a Results Only Learning Environment. In my school, report cards are issued four times per year. These are the only grades my students receive, and, as you know from the introduction, they give themselves these quarterly marks. Think back for a moment about poor Sasha and how she painfully decided on her *F*. When I briefly summarize our summer reading project, I begin explaining how evaluation works.

With as much clarity as possible for the beginning of a new school year, I emphasize that a results-only classroom is founded on three important words: *production*, *feedback*, and *change*. Rather than hand in a project and get it back with a 70/100 and a *C* grade, I show students how they will receive meaningful narrative feedback on everything they produce. This narrative feedback is the backbone of a results-only class. "Once you receive my feedback," I explain, "you are to make any changes I suggest and resubmit the activity for further evaluation and final comments." This, I tell them, is real teaching and learning—far better than the numbers or letters they are used to receiving. This approach gives students a real chance at mastery learning.

When my students leave on the first day of school, many scratch their heads in confusion, but it is good confusion. They have not seen a list of Dos and Don'ts, and they have not been given any expectations. They've learned about a low-pressure class that comes without the burden of homework, tests, and grades but with the amazing gift of autonomy—something truly rare and unknown to them. They've met an unorthodox teacher who comes across as a bit of a rebel—someone who, in their eyes, lives by a different set of rules. This is someone they like and maybe even respect. They've learned about a Results Only Learning Environment, and although they may not quite understand it, I find that they're certainly willing to give it a try.

2

Tapping into
Intrinsic Motivation

We have always been told to have motivation, but this type is different. Traditionally, motivation means studying for tests and doing homework on your own time. Yes, this requires independent motivation, but not to the extent that a Results Only Learning Environment does. The type of motivation we are expected to achieve in this environment occurs both in and out of the class. It's built out of trust and freedom. At first, it confused us because we had never been trusted quite like this. Initially, I thought my classmates would abuse the trust, but instead, I saw it made them more motivated to do their work. I think it was the fact that a teacher treated us as though we were adults. What teenager wouldn't want that? As we began doing projects, we learned how feedback worked. I loved the idea of knowing exactly what I did wrong and how I could fix it. Many of my classmates would agree when I say that we long for specific feedback in all of our classes. Overall, in our Language Arts class, we live and breathe intrinsic motivation. We aren't forced to do anything; we truly do it for learning's sake. That's what it's all about. Years from now, I will use the lessons and strategies I have learned in this environment to achieve excellence in academic and extracurricular aspects of my life. Results-only learning was a truly meaningful and nourishing experience in my life. I will never forget it.

—Elizabeth Bullock, 8th grade ROLE student

In a results-only classroom, it is critical for the teacher to encourage intrinsic motivation. In fact, this is probably the single most important component of a ROLE. It's not enough to simply define it for students and tell them to work hard and seek learning for learning's sake, even though this is the ultimate goal. Intrinsic motivation has to be taught, retaught, and emphasized from the first day of school until the last. In a ROLE, this begins with the mantra "production, feedback, change." Students must value narrative feedback as an extension of in-class lessons. They can then take that feedback and change the activity, improving upon it. Once students begin to approach learning this way, they no longer look for or expect points, percentages, or letter grades on their projects and activities. They begin to care only about the final results, which is what this type of education is all about.

You may think that teaching something to be intrinsic is a contradiction in terms. Nevertheless, even though intrinsic motivation comes from within, young people need a little coaching to find it. While my students work on the summer reading project mentioned earlier, I immediately begin my evaluation and feedback, which are key instruments to help them find the motivation that already exists inside them. At the same time, we work on a classroom website that hosts individual sites where students can create multiple pages and post just about any activity or class-related content they wish. The Feedback Toolkit (see Chapter 6) demonstrates how the use of student websites and other web-based tools plays an integral role in the results-only classroom. For now, though, it's important to know that the initial reading project is created on student websites, which is where I post the first narrative feedback students see.

Finding the Motivation Within

Since most students enter my class expecting activities to be worth set point values that ultimately compose the letter grades that go on their report cards, they waste no time looking for this kind of response to their work. Many ask how they did on part of a project before moving on to the next section. I tell them to read my feedback, which comes almost immediately after they complete each section. After quizzical looks, they forge ahead with questions such as, "Okay, but what do you think my score will be?" I remind them that there is no score—only the feedback.

Even though it is an individual project, students naturally progress at different rates, and I eventually have students coach one another. "Lisa just finished the part you're working on," I might tell a struggling student. "Why don't you show her the feedback I gave you, ask her some questions about how she did it, and see if you can figure it out together." This simple strategy lays the first bricks of the foundation of the results-only classroom. Now, two students are working toward a common goal, and they are focusing on my narrative feedback and attempting to improve part of a major project, with no promise of an extrinsic reward.

Although you may have used cooperative strategies such as this one throughout your teaching career, what's important to recognize here is the connection to the results-only system. Like blowing on the embers of a fire to arouse the flame, the idea of improving a project without the promise of a grade helps to fan the intrinsic motivation inside each student. When you explain the value of this cooperation to each student—or maybe even to the entire class—they begin to see that they can complete projects and, in fact, learn without the teacher's direct assistance, and they can do it without a grade. With continued emphasis on this type of cooperation, along with continual feedback-fueled change in an attempt to improve the project, students begin to want to learn on their own. When students learn without my help, only then do I feel like I've taught them something.

Year-Long Projects and Intrinsic Motivation

The results-only classroom is project based. Projects not only foster and enhance a sense of community and collaboration but also have a profound impact on intrinsic motivation. It's important to have at least one year-long project that students can work on occasionally (but intensively) in class and as a backdrop to other activities. A well-crafted year-long project will incentivize students to continue to improve it, even if it's not always part of the curriculum or being graded. People are inspired to complete many projects that have absolutely no extrinsic reward. People who contribute to open-source applications, such as Wikipedia, do so strictly for the intrinsic value—a sense of mastery and purpose (Pink, 2009). To further underscore this concept, Thom Markham, president of Global Redesigns, says, "The power of mastery achievement is a natural state of being. People enjoy doing tasks well, and [they] feel an intrinsic reward that perpetuates a spiral of further achievement" (2011, para. 3). With this notion in mind, very early in the school year, I introduce one of our year-long projects, which also happens to be the focal point of many of the lessons I'll teach as the year progresses.

Our Reading All Year (RAY) project encourages students to read at least 25 books by the end of the school year. If you recall, I teach 8th grade, and a large portion of my students enter my class having never read a book on their own. Therefore, when I announce that I want them to read 25 books, many students literally say, "That's crazy." The RAY project is inspired by concepts outlined in Donalyn Miller's *The Book Whisperer* (2009) and Nancie Atwell's *The Reading Zone* (2007). Miller and Atwell assert that when students are given the freedom to choose their own books—with some guidance from the teacher—even the most reluctant readers begin to acquire a love of books. Rather than demand summary writing, tests, and quizzes, teachers ask students to reflect on what they read in a variety of ways, including free writes and discussions with teachers and with peers. Brief lessons on story elements and the structure of nonfiction texts help students become comfortable applying these concepts to what they read.

The Reading All Year project includes several month-long reading workshops in which a wide variety of minilessons on reading strategies, figurative language, vocabulary acquisition, and book structure are taught. The project continues throughout the year without any extrinsic motivation, such as rewards, signed reading logs, or points and letter grades. Most evaluation and feedback occurs during the reading workshops when students complete written reflections, book talks, small-group book chats, reviews posted online, blog posts, and other activities related to their reading. There are never any traditional, carrot-and-stick assessments.

"Teachers who help kids act as readers learn how to assess their growth in ways that match what readers do: in a nutshell, the teachers talk with young readers, and they listen to them" (Atwell, 2007, p. 17). The aforementioned reflections, book talks, and other reading activities are used at the end of the grading period in the students' self-evaluations, when they decide on their final report card grade (more on this in Chapter 7). The activities that accompany independent reading might be considered extrinsic motivators by traditionalists. All students continue reading after the initial reading workshop, and they do this, at first, based on a desire to reach the original goal. This is, on the surface, much more of an extrinsic reward than a report card grade. As the year progresses, however, students continue to read because of the intrinsic value that reading carries. Most, in fact, read far beyond the original goal of 25 books (one year, a student read 93 novels).

No matter how little reading experience students may have had at the beginning of the year, most of my students end up reading constantly, without additional feedback or rewards (other than celebrating completed books). I believe this is directly tied to the discovery of intrinsic motivating factors that had always existed inside them but had not yet been awakened. This is perhaps the most complex part of results-only learning. There are few specific strategies for encouraging this "fanning," as I like to call it, of intrinsic motivation, other than those mentioned as part of our RAY project:

1. Setting goals
2. Celebrating success
3. Stating the value of a learning activity

To further illustrate the role that projects play in coaching intrinsic values, let me share another year-long project with a few examples of how students use it to demonstrate learning. Whereas the reading project encourages constant reading and the development of literacy skills, our year-long diary writing project enhances both fundamental writing skills and creativity. The project requires students to choose a specific historical period and create a character who might have lived during that time. (This is the autonomy piece.) Students write diary entries from the character's point of view, taking the opportunity to explore the historical period they've chosen. The minilessons that accompany this diary project meet many standards for writing, without segmenting writing into a single unit of study. Getting away from teaching in units is another facet of results-only learning. As the year progresses, students' writing develops and matures through their diary entries, ongoing feedback is provided from me and from student peers, and diary entries are continually edited, revised, and developed. After two or three weeks of an intense workshop setting, the class will move on to something else, but students will continue to work on their diary projects independently.

Working Without Carrots and Sticks

I tell students that they should continue to build their diary projects as the year continues and that I'll check in on their work periodically and leave ongoing feedback. If they read my comments regularly and use that feedback as individual instruction, they'll be able to improve their writing exponentially over the course of the school year.

"If all goes as planned," I explain, "you may create something truly excellent, perhaps even publishable." Remember two of the previously mentioned strategies for encouraging intrinsic motivation: goal-setting and stating the value of an activity. Encouraging the constant improvement of writing in order to make it publishable employs both of these strategies; it sets a goal and highlights the value of excellence in writing. Like with the reading project, the only reward associated with the diary project is the completion of a written work. Both projects represent major accomplishments for young readers and writers.

Notice that I'm not throwing points or letter grades at completed books or diary entries, yet the work continues. "Unfortunately, grades are generally an account of points earned through various activities that are influenced by artificial deadlines, grade inflation, extra credit, and subjectivity. It's time for us to change the student mind-set currently focused on reaching a particular percentage and instead empower them to take charge of their learning and measure their own success" (Kuntz, 2012, p. 3). My students have no promise of a high grade or threat of a low one. There are no phone calls home if the production stops. I constantly remind them that reading and writing will improve their lives in every way. They are special, I say, because they are reading and writing more than most middle school students across the United States. Every finished book is a major accomplishment that we celebrate, and every diary entry is the continuation of something unique that exemplifies who they are as storytellers.

How Feedback Fans Intrinsic Motivation

Students become motivated by the results they see in their own work. The proof is in the feedback. Not only do I provide comments, but students constantly respond to those comments and provide me with valuable feedback—this is part of the formative assessment discussed later that is so crucial to the success of the results-only classroom. What follows are actual examples of feedback, left as comments on student websites, from the diary project.

> **Mr. Barnes:** Amber, I like your project so far. You are telling a very thought-provoking story. Some entries should be broken up, as they are a bit long. Also, check your facts; you mention Susan B. Anthony in an entry dated 1917. Anthony died in 1906. Well done overall, thus far, though.

> **Amber:** Thanks for your feedback. I really needed it.

Imagine getting a "thanks" from a student for a comment you left on a project that is worth no points and has no grade. The next example includes specific instructions for incorporating vocabulary, based on an earlier minilesson. This is the Redirect part of the feedback system I call Summarize, Explain, Redirect, and Resubmit (SE2R), which is explored in detail in Chapter 5.

> **Mr. Barnes:** Melissa, I love your story. Your character seems very real, with real emotion. Your writing is solid. Be careful, though, to proofread each entry. For example, I saw this run-on in one of the early entries: "I heard a rumbling sound, I knew what was coming." This is a focus area for us, so be sure to correct it. Also, I'd like to see you start putting some of our vocabulary from either our vocab book or our literature book into your entries. Be sure to highlight these, if you do.

> **Melissa:** Mr. Barnes, I made the corrections. Please check them.

> **Mr. Barnes:** Excellent corrections, Melissa. I see that you took the revising task seriously. You didn't just change one little detail, but you made plenty of significant changes. Your highlighted vocabulary is well-chosen and properly used.

In the traditional classroom, a specific assignment that calls for something such as vocabulary integration or proper use of punctuation would likely receive a set point value or a grade. The teacher's assessment might include a simple comment, noting what was done incorrectly, and a final grade, which would be entered into a grade book. In the above examples, Amber and Melissa might have received a *B* or a 40/50, and we would then move to the next assignment, with no further follow-up on this one. Amber and Melissa would either accept the grade and say nothing or they might complain that the assessment was unfair for one reason or another. Most likely, they'd simply shrug and move on to the next activity, caring very little about the mistakes they made.

The results-only classroom, conversely, encourages learning and fans the intrinsic motivation that lies within each student, rather than smother it with a punitive grade. Amber and Melissa are influenced by the positive feedback and the changes I suggest, because they see the recommendations as constructive and useful for learning. Amber and Melissa want to improve their work—to make it publishable—so they look at the narrative feedback as coaching, and they willingly improve their writing. This sort of results-only teaching and learning ignites passion in students, which is a critical part of education that is often missing in traditional classrooms. "When we have a high level of passion in the material, it makes the information and content come alive and stirs the interest of our learners" (Maiers & Sandvold, 2011, p. 30). Amber and Melissa are excellent examples of this kind of passion.

3

Letting Go of Homework
and Worksheets

For me, the Results Only Learning Environment was a place where I could learn at my own pace, and that was great. It is much different from a student's perspective, because you've grown used to a traditional classroom environment. Everything seems very loose and easy, as opposed to having exact deadlines and home assignments every night. Of course, any child who hears of a teacher who gives no homework will be thrilled. For me, and many other students, you begin to get over that initial feeling soon, and you want to take the initiative and learn on your own. A child deciding his or her own grade may seem crazy, but it was really great for me, because I felt I was in control of getting the grade I deserved based on the overall work I did. From my experience, I believe if you jump into it with an open mind, a ROLE can be suitable for any classroom. It may seem different at first, but I have taken from the experience that it is a great method for learning.
—Ava Glessner, 7th grade ROLE student

When Cali Ressler and Jody Thompson were leading teams at Best Buy during the mid-2000s, they gave their employees the equivalent of the homework and worksheets that traditional teachers give to their students. Those assignments demanded particular activities that had to be done in specific increments of time each day. Best Buy was headed for massive expansion, and Ressler and Thompson had concerns. Their anxiety prompted a change that completely revolutionized how employees at the electronic gadget giant complete their work. The idea was simple yet brilliant. Rather than evaluate daily performance on hours worked, Ressler and Thompson decided to create a Results Only Work Environment (ROWE)—an environment where performance is evaluated on completed tasks rather than on when and how the task was completed. Many Best Buy corporate employees set their own hours and continue to complete projects at home or in the office after most other workers are gone for the day. Some leave early, whereas others begin at noon and work late. With the ROWE system fully entrenched, absenteeism at Best Buy has plummeted by a remarkable 45 percent (NewWOW, 2011).

During the all-important summer when my teaching philosophy changed, I contacted the creators of ROWE to get their opinions about possibly applying the system to the K–12 classroom. A few days later, I received a response that indicated Ressler and Thompson loved the idea of results-only learning, and they invited me to share my progress implementing the results-only system. With my commitment validated, it was time to initiate the ROLE with my students. This meant eliminating many of the old methods I had been conditioned to use during most of my first 16 years as a classroom teacher. Unlike Ressler and Thompson's ROWE, I couldn't allow my students to come to class when they wanted; we still had to operate within the confines of the scheduled day (although this is another part of a traditional school that I'd like to see eliminated).

Deciding when to work, though, was only part of the results-only concept. I realized that Ressler and Thompson had other philosophies I could apply to a K–12 environment. The primary function of ROWE is to give workers autonomy—the ability to complete projects without too much supervision. It was this decision-making power that I wanted to bring to my classroom. Even if I couldn't tell my students to set their own hours during the school day, I could give them more freedom while they were there, accompanied by the power to decide how to work, both in and out of class. This meant a complete overhaul of daily in-class and out-of-class procedures.

Throwing Out Tradition

Homework has been a staple of U.S. education as far back as the stereotypical one-room schoolhouse. Its effectiveness is rarely given a second thought. Preservice teachers are instructed to assign homework, and the habit is perpetuated. If you want to create a results-only classroom, however, you will have to commit to changing your approach to homework. There is no shortage of opinions about homework—both for and against it—so I won't spend much ink here adding to the existing research. I would, though, recommend Alfie Kohn's *The Homework Myth* (2006b) as one of the most thorough volumes of work on the subject and as a treatise on what a monumental waste of time and energy traditional homework is at most grade levels. Kohn cites the work of dozens of researchers who demonstrate few or no connections between homework and achievement, and he references the work of renowned Duke University psychologist and education professor Harris Cooper, who has spent decades attempting to link homework to academic success. Kohn systematically debunks Cooper's work, demonstrating how, in recent studies, Cooper questions his early research and begins to wonder about the real value of homework, especially in the primary grades. School districts as large as the Los Angeles Unified School District are beginning to see the innumerable problems with homework and are dramatically changing their policies, significantly reducing the impact it can have on students' grades (Stansbury, 2011). Reducing homework, though, is only the beginning. As you continue reading, you'll quickly see there is no room for traditional homework in a ROLE.

For my part, I began phasing homework out of my class the year I had "the bad bunch." In a failed attempt to help these students pass my class, I assigned less homework in the belief that since most of them weren't completing it, it was turning into something that was only lowering their grades. As I dove deeper into the research, I realized that my decision to decrease homework was the right one, even if my reasoning for it was flawed. Homework serves no function in a results-only classroom—not just because it punishes students with constant zeroes but also because it doesn't fit into the project-based, choice-driven nature of a ROLE.

The first goal of a results-only system is to create a sense of autonomy. I want my students to demonstrate learning through projects they complete over time. Traditional homework, which mostly requires note taking, text work, and rote memorization, is not effective in project-based learning. This doesn't mean my students never work outside of class. They do, but they always choose when to do so and what kind of work to complete. They choose to read nightly because I've challenged them to read at least 25 books during the school year and because we've discussed the value of reading in general. They meet with their peers and work on year-long projects because they are motivated to create something unique. Their personal investments in the projects encourage them to work outside of class.

Without getting too much into the homework debate, let me emphasize that one of the many inherent problems with homework is that it does not encourage autonomy. The most effective teachers tell students that their opinions are important. If we follow this declaration with "do-this-and-do-it-this-way" homework assignments, then the message becomes muddied, and any trust that has been established with students is eroded.

The Homework Challenge

Transitioning from traditional homework assignments to a project-based, student-driven method may sound difficult or even impossible. As previously stated, I eased into this transition, and you may need to do the same, especially if you are a veteran teacher who has been assigning nightly homework. If you question the validity of dramatically changing your approach to homework, let me share a way to simplify the transition by giving you a challenge. This challenge will cure most of your ingrained "I-have-to-assign-homework" ailments and is based on my earlier assertion (borrowed from Kohn) that there are few if any connections between homework and academic achievement.

Prior to taking this challenge, ask yourself why you assign homework. When I ask teachers this simple question, 90 percent of them respond the same way: "Homework provides practice and preparation for tests and quizzes." Therefore, for the sake of the homework challenge, let's assume that this is the primary reason that teachers assign homework. Setting up the challenge is easy, if you are willing to stop assigning homework for one unit of study. Every teacher can change even his or her favorite instructional routine for two to four weeks.

Be sure to select a unit that has existing assessments. I use numerous web-based diagnostic tools, some of which I've had for years, so taking the challenge was easy for me. Of course, you can also use a hard copy test or quiz. Teach the unit as you have during previous years, using the same activities, direct instruction, visual aids, and teaching strategies you've used in the past. The key to the challenge, as you've likely guessed, is that you have to assign no homework. Absolutely none. If going over homework in class the following day is part of the unit, then simply replace that time with more in-class practice activities, enrichment, or small-group discussion (the best choice in a ROLE). At the end of the unit, give students the same assessment you've used in the past.

An honest evaluation of the challenge can be done in one of two ways. If you are taking this challenge well into the school year, then you'll already have data on your current students. You will know how they typically perform on assessments, and you'll know which students consistently turn in homework and which do not. My guess is that the students who consistently complete homework assignments will have done well on prior assessments, and they are likely your best students in terms of grades. (I know this sounds like I'm contradicting myself, but please bear with me.) I don't have to quote research to tell you that students who complete their assignments typically get good grades in school, and those who do not complete assignments usually get poor grades. (This is the problem with grades, a subject I'll dissect later.)

I'm not suggesting that eliminating homework has a bigger effect, when it comes to test results, on low-achieving students than it does on high-achieving students. In fact, what you'll likely see in most cases is very little change. Many of your students will score within the same range as they have throughout the year, and any changes likely will be positive. Typically, the homework challenge yields slight increases for low achievers because they are more confident; they have not been repeatedly beaten down by poor grades—due to missed homework assignments—throughout the unit. Students who have previously scored well on tests will score well this time too, clearly demonstrating that they don't need the additional nightly practice.

Before discussing the results of the challenge, let's consider the second way to evaluate it. If you are taking the homework challenge at the beginning of the school year, you won't have test data on your students. You can still take the challenge if you have a beginning-of-the-year unit from which you're comfortable eliminating homework. Be sure, though, to choose something for which you would normally give nightly homework or the challenge results will be skewed. Be sure also to teach the unit exactly as you have in prior years—just without homework. The difference here is you must compare your current students' test results with those from students you taught in previous years. Granted, there may be students in the two groups with different ability levels, but this won't affect the big picture as you are only deciding if homework has affected the outcome. You don't need to dig up old test results. This is a fairly informal challenge, and you are certainly insightful enough to know how students have done on a particular unit test in the past. If the class averages were around 80 percent, then use this number as a guide.

Obviously, the first method of evaluation (in the middle of the year) is better, but don't let the time of year stop you from taking this important challenge, especially if you're seriously considering creating a ROLE. Remember, the critical information that this challenge provides is whether your students need homework to improve their academic achievement, as measured on a unit test. If some students' scores decline slightly and others increase slightly, then the challenge has successfully demonstrated that homework is unnecessary. To put a finer point on this, let me share my own challenge results.

When I began teaching in a results-only classroom, I needed to prove to myself that it was truly effective. Although I'm not a fan of multiple-choice assessments, I had several from prior years, which made it easy to test my growing assumption that homework was not connected to achievement. I decided to use a web-based assessment—allowing me to get immediate feedback. We were beginning a unit on short fiction, which involved vocabulary skills and literary terms. In the past, I had used vocabulary worksheets and short written responses for nightly homework during the short story unit. At the end of this three-week unit, we took a test. In two prior years, the test scores were abysmal. The year of "the bad bunch," five classes averaged 71 percent on the short fiction/vocabulary assessment. One class was as low as 65 percent, and the highest scoring group came in at 78 percent. When the unit ended, I recorded those results in the grade book, and we moved forward, away from short fiction.

In the results-only classroom, we revisited some lessons based on the diagnostic results and retook the assessment if the results demonstrated a lack of understanding. This is a key element of teaching and learning that I had left out in the past. The results of the new diagnostic, which eliminated homework and worksheets and used ROLE strategies such as paired analysis, student-directed concept checks, and small-group discussions, were astounding. My five classes averaged 88 percent—a whopping 17 percent increase over the prior groups that took the same assessment. Keep in mind that these scores came with absolutely no homework. Your own homework challenge may not yield such remarkable results, but remember, even if there is no change at all when you compare your challenge test to prior scores, you will see that homework is a waste of valuable learning time. I believe my students' scores were much higher not only because of the lack of a negative impact from homework but also because of the other previously mentioned elements of a Results Only Learning Environment.

Worksheets Don't Work

I stopped using the word *worksheet* years ago while I was still hammering students with pointless assignments. I simply didn't like the implication of the word, and I was constantly trying to convince students that it wasn't work. Of course, they knew it definitely was work. A successful results-only classroom is free from worksheets and the harm they cause. Among other things, worksheets have been proven to waste valuable class time and focus on teaching only rote skills (Volante, 2004). Most important, though, is that worksheets make students hate learning. If you don't believe me, simply ask your students, "Hey, do you guys like this worksheet? Do you think it helps you learn the material?"

I'm sure you know in your heart what the answer will be even before you ask.

Perhaps you think that the in-class activities you assign are *not* worksheets. Let's find out, before we explore better methods of teaching and learning in a results-only classroom. In the previous section, I asked you to take the homework challenge. Here is another challenge, although this one does not involve evaluating your students. This challenge is so simple that you can do it in seconds. Just go to your file cabinet or textbook supplement or anything else from which you might assign an in-class activity. The challenge now is to decide if what you select is a worksheet. The following questions make up my worksheet litmus test:

1. Does the activity come from a source with the word *workbook* or *lesson* on it?
2. Was the activity copied from a textbook?
3. Does the activity look like a multiple-choice quiz?
4. Does the activity require students to fill in a blank space by copying information found in a textbook?
5. Do you currently call or have you ever called the activity a worksheet?

If you answer *yes* to any of these questions, then you have a worksheet on your hands, and you need to take serious action. I'm attempting to inject a little levity here, but the message is a serious one. Students do, in fact, hate worksheets. Worksheets, workbooks, practice tests, or any other canned assignments—pretending to be something other than worksheets—bore students and make them hate learning. These assignments turn average teachers into weak ones and undermine the efforts of potentially brilliant teachers. Worksheets are crutches, used primarily as tools to teach to a test, and this creates a vicious cycle of bad education.

The cycle roughly follows this pattern. A science teacher has a unit on weather. She has a final test that she's been using for years. She has workbook lessons that require basic rote memorization, so her students can answer the questions on the test. The students have no choice in how they learn about weather. They complete worksheets, maybe review them, and then regurgitate information from the worksheets when they take the test. A typical bell curve shows that 20 percent receive *As* (because they know the system), 20 percent fail (because they didn't complete the worksheets or review for the test), and 60 percent land somewhere in the middle (because they know how to do just enough to get by). What hasn't happened here is real learning. Replace the worksheets and workbooks with web tools, hands-on activities, interviews with relevant experts or professionals, videos, and small-group discussions, and the students will learn about weather. Both the worksheets and the test can be discarded.

The Research

The Results Only Learning Environment employs only the best parts of research by a variety of experts—all of whom vilify worksheets and similar tools in one way or another. Mark Forget, the creator of MAX Teaching, believes that when it comes to classroom learning activities, cooperation is king. Forget has developed numerous strategies that involve collaboration and summarizing techniques to improve learning (Forget, 2004). Stephen Krashen, who has studied reading literacy for more than 40 years, also believes that traditional strategies, such as guided reading and teaching writing skills in isolation, are ineffective. Krashen has found that a wide exposure to books and intense individual reading dramatically increase literacy skills (Krashen, 2011b).

Intense voluntary, independent reading eliminates the need for the worksheets and workbooks that many reading teachers use. College professors Richard Allington and Rachael Gabriel have studied effective and ineffective reading practices across the United States, and they offer a variety of strategies for better reading and increased learning, all of which shun the use of worksheets and working on skills in isolation. In fact, Allington and Gabriel very pointedly say that teachers should "eliminate almost all worksheets and workbooks" (2012, p. 14).

Once we recognize that leading education researchers suggest that basic note-taking, guided reading, and rote memorization activities do not increase student achievement, it's time to reconsider the value of worksheets and workbooks in every classroom. This then leads to the following question: How do we provide useful instruction and practice without something that's been the centerpiece of classrooms for so long?

Minilessons and Engaging Learning Activities

For much of my teaching career, note taking and worksheets were commonplace in my classroom. On a typical day, students would copy parts of speech, comma rules, or literary elements, which were beamed onto a dusty screen or yellowed wall by an antique overhead projector. This was followed by a very old worksheet, including stray pencil marks or coffee stains on each photocopy. The worksheet might contain sentences with instructions for students to label the parts of speech. Another might ask students to place proper punctuation in a series of sentences. Yet another assignment, slightly improved but still bad enough to make the most enthusiastic students cringe, instructed weary learners to read a paragraph and identify the similes and metaphors. Only the latter worksheet has even a speck of higher-level thinking— encouraging students to apply a basic understanding of figurative language to written text. I could create a handy multiple-choice quiz or test on any combination of these awful lessons and drills, and the results might be acceptable. Alternatively, the quiz might be a complete disaster, because students were so bored by the lessons and accompanying activities that they would forget the material as soon as they left the classroom. Either way, not much learning took place.

A results-only system uses much better instructional methods, and the concepts are internalized by students because of a combination of choice, movement, and fun. The last concept—fun—should be as important as the first two. As education researchers Russ Quaglia and Kristine Fox write, "The condition of fun and excitement and the process of learning are not strangers. Rather, they live side by side and depend on each other for sustenance" (2003, p. 53). Take note of this symbiotic relationship between learning and fun in the activities and projects included throughout this book. To illustrate how to eliminate horrible worksheets, such as the ones alluded to earlier, it's important to begin with better instructional strategies.

The minilessons in a ROLE do away with the overhead projector and all forms of lecture. In their place are brief videos, podcasts, screencasts, social media, web tools, and mobile learning devices (more on technology integration in Chapter 4). Therefore, when I want students to learn literary terms, the instruction might begin with a list of words on my classroom website. Instead of providing students with definitions to copy, as I might have done in the past, I tell students to find the definitions on their own, using any of the tools at their fingertips. The only rule for the lesson is they can't leave the classroom. This activity becomes fun in a hurry.

"Can I text someone for the answer?" one student asks.

"Definitely," I say. "Just make sure it's a reliable source and not a peer in another class." Although few students pursue this route, this can be a wonderful, interactive activity that engages even the most disinterested learner.

Another student asks if she can use the Internet on her smartphone. I can't see why not.

"What about a textbook?"

"Boring!" I announce to a smattering of laughs. "But I'm sure you'll find some of the words there."

"Is it okay to ask students in other groups?" someone wonders.

"Hmm, intergroup communication?" I think aloud. "If you feel that's useful, go for it."

Soon, my classroom is bustling, and all I've done is combine instruction and activity, without ever pulling out a worksheet or asking students to copy anything. "Whether it be for the sake of the linkages between movement and memory, or for the sake of gender or other learner differences, the use of movement within your lessons can enhance learning for your students while providing you with evidence of active participation and cognitive engagement" (Himmele & Himmele, 2011, p. 59). As students scurry about, in search of discovery, some remain seated, deciding to write definitions in a notebook. (Remember, I don't instruct them to do this; they choose to do so.) Others type entries on their personal page of the classroom website. Still others move from group to group, trading information, like eager stock brokers buying and selling futures on Wall Street. It doesn't really matter what method students use, because they are all learning. They choose how to get the information and how to absorb it.

If this activity can be called work, then the students are the ones doing it. In fact, I've done far less than any traditional teacher would have done while trying to meet the same learning outcomes. No time is wasted creating a visual aid or typing and photocopying a worksheet. The learning that takes place is truly inspirational, and evaluation is easy and unobtrusive. I've even videotaped my students as they complete this one-day project. I interrupt them briefly and share the video, which I quickly upload to the classroom website from my smartphone. "What do you notice?" I like to ask. "Johnny's having a bad hair day," the class clown will shout, garnering plenty of laughter. Invariably, someone says, "Everyone is working" or "People are getting the information in a lot of different ways." This is a perfect opportunity to reinforce the ongoing effectiveness of the ROLE.

I can extend this activity by asking students to apply what they've learned to one or more of our year-long projects. Consider the diary writing and Reading All Year projects for a moment. This vocabulary discovery activity can be a lesson that is applied all year in both diary entries and reading reflections. Students can infuse figurative language into their writing. They can create web-based storyboards that demonstrate irony, theme, conflict, hyperbole, and much more. What makes this truly powerful is that the learning outcomes are mastered through yearlong applications. Learning becomes less compartmentalized into one-and-done units. As students internalize the concepts, learning becomes less compartmentalized into one-and-done units because the concepts are applied to various activities and projects throughout the school year. This is one reason students in a ROLE typically outperform their traditional classroom peers on standardized tests, even though results-only teachers never teach to the test.

4

Teaching the ROLE Way

The way I think of the Results Only Learning Environment is that it's all about being in control of my own education. I have had Mr. Barnes for language arts in both 7th and 8th grades, so I know how he "ROLEs," but for the students who haven't had him as long as I have, catching on to his teaching techniques is simple and fun. One of my favorite parts of the way we are taught is the feedback we get after completing a task, given to us on the smart board in class or on Mr. Barnes's blog. He doesn't have to badger students for their worksheets or workbook lessons, because there aren't any. Just about everything is web-based.

When I receive feedback on my assignments, I feel like I have accomplished something. Whether I do poorly or I succeed, I have the chance to go back to whatever it was and redo it. Then, all I have to do is message Mr. Barnes or email him. At the end of each quarter, students evaluate themselves on what they have completed throughout the year, and they put a letter grade on it. Yes, you read it right. Students give themselves a grade! Up until the end of each quarter there are no grades; there's only feedback. I know from experience what it's like to give myself a grade, and it's not always going to be an A+, if that's not how I progressed. I think it would be rather intriguing to see other core classes like science, math, or social studies try using a ROLE as their method of teaching, because it's definitely my favorite!

—Chaitlyn Dubay, 8th grade ROLE student

It is my hope that the simple strategies outlined in this chapter will convince you to finally leave homework and worksheets behind. Like many veteran teachers, I had yellowed worksheets and daily routines that made me feel comfortable, yet they bored my students into submission or, worse, into disruption. When you have to deal with classroom management, parents, administrators, and the myriad of unexpected stressors that may arise on any given day, routines and worksheets become a welcome escape. Canned units and activities essentially make quick work of the academic portion of your day. The shift to a ROLE is not an easy one. What you'll love about this system, though, is how these strategies simplify many of the difficulties noted earlier, such as classroom rules and consequences and the creation of worksheets, homework assignments, and unit tests. Best of all, you can apply ROLE strategies to any subject or grade. There are only five strategies, but they are multifaceted and require time, energy, and repetition. Once you've put results-only learning initiatives into your classroom and demonstrated their value to your students, a life-changing transformation will take place.

Strategy 1: Incorporate the Year-Long Project

I've had colleagues who contend that project-based learning avoids specific content—that it does not address actual skills. Research indicates otherwise. Project-based learning "marries the teaching of critical thinking skills with rich content, because students need something to think critically about—it cannot be taught independent of content" (Larmer, 2011, para. 4). The year-long project in the results-only classroom bears out Larmer's assertion. When done right, the year-long project covers most learning outcomes and encourages higher-level thinking. In addition, it helps eliminate the dull routines we were taught to use back in our preservice days. This can be frightening to many teachers who fear a loss of control. Even though the ROLE is built on freedom and a little chaos, the year-long project maintains a sense of structure and routine that will help make your classroom run smoothly. "For teachers only used to direct instruction, it may be challenging at first to manage students working in teams and handle the open-endedness of PBL, but with more experience it gets easier" (Larmer, 2011, para. 9).

A year-long project can be anything; it just needs to be subject-related and something that can incorporate minilessons throughout the year. The project should include elements that students can work on every day (see Figure 4.1). What makes the year-long project so successful is that it is fundamental to the results-only philosophy that the teacher works all year to cultivate. If the project is discussed and celebrated constantly, and if there is enough freedom of choice in it to create a legitimate sense of ownership in each student, it will become an integral part of a project-based class, and your students will come to believe in it. Remember, by coaching intrinsic motivation, you teach your students to set long-term goals and value production. "Human beings work harder—on behalf of themselves or others—when they have a goal. The goal must be relevant to the person's needs and desires" (Markham, 2011, para. 3).

As the school year moves forward and students see their goals being met and their work evolving, they will hunger for more time to work on their projects. The social bookmarking project in Figure 4.1 demonstrates how students can surf the Internet (something they love to do) and choose nonfiction articles that relate to novels they are reading, which they have also selected as part of our Reading All Year project. The web tool Diigo provides a powerful platform for students to demonstrate understanding of the novels since they can connect the content to relevant real-world information. I can leave narrative feedback on Diigo, as can peers, which makes this an amazing online learning community. Diigo, like most social media tools, has a variety of safety protocols that make this a secure community for learners.

4.1 | Year-Long Project Guidelines

OVERVIEW: Diigo is a tool that will play an instrumental role in our Reading All Year (RAY) project. To supplement the books you read for our 2,500 book challenge, you will also read articles and blog posts on the Internet that relate in some way to the topics, themes, or characters in your books. Sharing content is a major part of how we learn, so you'll be helping your peers, as well. Diigo, and our Diigo class group, provides the perfect tool for summarizing and sharing information.

YOUR TASK: For each book you read, locate at least one Internet article that contains relevant information. For example, if I'm reading Will Hobbs's *Go Big or Go Home*, I might locate, tag, and annotate an article on meteorites, since the novel is about how a meteorite affects the main character who finds it. The annotation (a brief summary) should explain how the article relates to the book. Learn more about tags and annotations in the Project Steps below and from the videos on our classroom web site.

PROJECT STEPS:

1. Begin by surfing the web for articles that contain interesting information that is related in some way to your book. It may take some time before you find an appropriate article. Be sure to read the articles in their entirety.

2. When you decide on the article that supplements your book, perform the following steps:

    A. Copy the web address of the article.

    B. Paste the web address into your class group bookmark section on Diigo.

    C. Choose an appropriate tag. All bookmarks should include a tag that is the author's last name. (For example, appropriate tags for my meteorite article would be *meteorites*, *Hobbs*, and *scifi* because the article is about meteorites and the book is a science fiction novel written by Will Hobbs.)

    D. Be sure your annotation is not taken verbatim from the website. Delete the comment that Diigo "pulls" in, and write your own detailed annotation. Be sure to explain how the article relates to your book.

    E. Read, bookmark, and annotate at least one article for each book you read throughout the year. This means you should have at least 25 bookmarks and annotations by the end of the year.

Because our Reading All Year project is such a huge part of what we do, my students look at it as an enjoyable task they constantly want to spend time on. If they enter class on a particular day and I don't immediately address them (I might be getting journals from our closet or writing something on our interactive whiteboard), then they open their books and begin reading or they talk quietly about their books or about books they intend to read later. If we've had three or four days of minilessons and small-group activities unrelated to our project, I may take a day and call it a free choice project day. Students decide what to work on, with the only expectation being that they do something related to the year-long project. With so many project threads, there is always something for students to do. If they are not reading or discussing books, they might be posting a reflection letter to the class blog, adding a bookmark to the class Diigo site, or updating their reading plans, which are maintained on another social network (goodreads.com). These are always good days that see plenty of significant work from all students. The year-long project reinforces the idea that people are driven by autonomy, mastery, and purpose (Pink, 2009). If the project is well designed, then students will feel as though they are creating something substantial, and they will want to develop it to the best of their ability. In fact, students enjoy the interactivity and autonomy so much that they often work after school and on weekends, improving their project work on our various websites.

Although the results-only classroom and the year-long project are built on autonomy, it's important to help students create checkpoint goals while providing a menu of project activities that help them master the learning outcomes. For example, in the beginning of the year, I teach novel structure. I might start with a discovery activity such as the one I discussed earlier on literary elements. Students then work in small groups with various books, and they discuss structure as they read. Alternatively, we may complete a short shared novel, and students summarize the structure of the book together. Since I want their year-long projects to demonstrate mastery of book structure, I create a menu of choices that help students show me what they know. Students value the lessons learned because they see them as part of something they'll use forever, and they weren't fed a stream of insignificant worksheets to learn them.

The directions for the project are simple: "Choose one item from each part of the menu to demonstrate the structure of three or more of your novels for this grading period." Notice the use of technology in the detailed instructions that follow this summary (see Figure 4.2). This allows students to share their projects with others and celebrate their successes. "Blogs and other Web 2.0 tools provide opportunities to receive recognition from peers beyond the classroom in ways students have never had before. Today's tools make it possible for students to publish work in a variety of media formats, which can have a powerful impact on student motivation" (Dean, Hubbell, Pitler, & Stone, 2012, p. 33). Many of these tools are represented in the menu of choices students have. After the summary directions, the project is broken into the categories of book structure that I want to evaluate in one grading period. Other elements of fiction (perhaps point of view, rising action, climax, and falling action) might appear in a later project. As you can see, this is an in-depth project, and we have only covered a quarter of it. Each marking period brings a new menu of choices for students. This allows them to demonstrate what they are doing during an entire year of reading. The ROLE's workshop setting (discussed in greater detail later in this chapter) gives students plenty of time to complete their projects. The many web tools they use fan the intrinsic motivation that drives students toward mastery learning.

Finally, the year-long project helps teachers work smarter rather than harder. Although much time will be spent on evaluation and feedback, year-long projects meet many Common Core State Standards

4.2 | Year-Long Project Guidelines

Character & Setting

- Create a post-it wall, using Wallwisher or a similar web-based tool, in which at least nine characters interact. Be sure that the dialogue makes your audience understand the characters and how they fit into the story.

- Create a poster, using Glogster, Automatoon, or plain cardboard, that contains at least nine characters from multiple books. The poster should include a drawing or graphic representation of the characters, along with several sentences that describe their role in the stories.

- Create your own character activity. (Discuss your idea with Mr. Barnes.)

Conflict & Theme

- Create one or more videos/movies, using YouTube, Animoto, Jing, or another web-based tool, in which you clearly demonstrate the conflicts, how those conflicts are resolved, and the key lessons in at least three books. Each video/movie should include a combination of pictures or animation and text.

- Create a series of brief podcasts (three or more) that clearly demonstrate the conflicts, how those conflicts are resolved, and the key lessons in at least three books. The podcasts may be character interviews, additional chapters, or anything else you think is important.

- Write a brief review for each of your books. Be sure your reviews outline the conflicts, how those conflicts are resolved, and the key lessons.

You and Your Books

- Using your favorite web tool, musical instrument, or a poster board, create something that is not necessarily related to book structure but connects you to any book you've read or are reading this grading period. Consider why the book is important to you and why you'll remember it forever. Be creative here. You may want to

  - Produce a song (using ujam or another web-based mixing tool).
  - Add a chapter.
  - Write a poem.
  - Produce a one-act play.
  - Deliver a monologue from a character's point of view.
  - Interview an author.
  - Come up with your own idea.

and learning outcomes (see Figure 4.3). Year-long projects also provide activities that engage students when the primary classroom teacher is absent or called away for meetings or other professional activities. Year-long project work provides a far better learning opportunity than any substitute teacher plan you could ever create. Substitute teachers, who cover for me when I'm out, often admit astonishment at how smoothly my classes run without me. They are amazed at the efficiency of the learning community and how my students work so well, both together and independently, with very little instruction. I always tell them that this has little to do with me. It's really just the power of the year-long project and the freedom of the results-only classroom.

Strategy 2: Talk Less

I'm sure this isn't the first time you've heard or read that lecturing to students of any age is a recipe for disaster, but even if you think you don't lecture, you should probably talk less than you do. I don't have empirical data on this, but I'm willing to bet that my class has less direct instruction than most middle school classes in any subject. Nevertheless, I still believe I talk too much. Teachers talk; it's simply in our nature. We give instructions—two or three times—because we don't think our students are listening. We repeat a concept over and over because three students had their heads down or weren't looking in our direction. We dwell on the same visual aid, talking about every bullet point, when the words and pictures of a well-crafted presentation usually say enough. We spend five minutes summing up, belaboring an earlier lesson for no good reason—other than to fill the time with sound. It's been reported that teachers ask the most questions in class on any given day. Do you know who answers the most questions? Teachers.

Education researcher John Hattie, who reviewed studies involving three million students, suggests that teachers spend 80 percent of class time talking, and they should "just shut up" (quoted in Stevenson,

4.3 | Common Core State Standards Mastered During a Year-Long Project

Key Ideas and Details

(CCSS.ELA–Literacy RL.8.1) Cite the textual evidence that most strongly supports an analysis of what the text says explicitly as well as inferences drawn from the text.

(CCSS.ELA–Literacy RL.8.2) Determine a theme or central idea of a text and analyze its development over the course of the text, including its relationship to the characters, setting, and plot; provide an objective summary of the text.

Craft and Structure

(CCSS.ELA–Literacy RL.8.4) Determine the meaning of words and phrases as they are used in a text, including figurative and connotative meanings; analyze the impact of specific word choices on meaning and tone, including analogies or allusions to other texts.

Integration of Knowledge and Ideas

(CCSS.ELA–Literacy RI.8.9) Analyze a case in which two or more texts provide conflicting information on the same topic and identify where the texts disagree on matters of fact or interpretation.

Range of Reading and Level of Text Complexity

(CCSS.ELA–Literacy RL.8.10) By the end of the year, read and comprehend literature, including stories, dramas, and poems, at the high end of grades 6–8 text complexity band independently and proficiently.

Research to Build and Present Knowledge

(CCSS.ELA–Literacy W.8.8) Gather relevant information from multiple print and digital sources, using search terms effectively; assess the credibility and accuracy of each source; and quote or paraphrase the data and conclusions of others while avoiding plagiarism and following a standard format for citation.

Comprehension and Collaboration

(CCSS.ELA–Literacy SL.8.1) Engage effectively in a range of collaborative discussions (one-on-one, in groups, and teacher-led) with diverse partners on grade 8 topics, texts, and issues, building on others' ideas and expressing their own clearly.

2011). Even when luminaries such as Hattie tell teachers that lecturing is an inefficient teaching strategy, teachers continue talking. Why? The answer is simple. Like those worn-out worksheets and tired daily routines, lecturing puts teachers in a safe zone. We're comfortable talking because we've done it for so long and because we were taught that this is what teaching looks like. We talk and students listen, even though we now know that they really don't listen. What happens when we stop talking? As you may have guessed, students start to talk and fill the silence, but this isn't necessarily a bad thing.

Teaching experts emphasize that people remember about 10 percent of what they read, 20 percent of what they hear (via lecture), and 30 percent of what they see. However, they remember an uncanny 70 percent of what is discussed (Forget, 2004). With this in mind, it seems as if students learn best when they share information in a cooperative setting—not when they passively listen to teachers. ROLE Strategy 2 covers this very succinctly: talk less. Obviously, there's more to this strategy; we have to replace the talking with something that is conducive to learning. Although this might be frightening, it shouldn't be. All you have to do is embrace the silence and let your students do the rest.

Most teachers struggle with their own silence. Questions must be answered, and if students aren't busy completing a worksheet, there must be talking. Sadly, students are usually forbidden to talk, unless they are asked to speak, because of a deep-seated fear of chaos. Well-placed silence, however, can be one of the most effective tools a results-only teacher has in his or her toolbox. When I feel that I'm talking too much, usually because I'm belaboring a point, I'll often just stop talking. This took some practice. At times, I literally tell my students that it's time for me to shut up. This elicits some quizzical looks and often some excellent discussion from students. They'll ask questions either to me or to one another. Sometimes, small-group debates ensue, and I just get out of the way and listen. This is exactly what Hattie suggests. When the teacher stops talking, he or she should walk around and listen (Stevenson, 2011). This is when some of the best student engagement takes place. Sound crazy? This is a results-only classroom. When the teacher stops talking, learning begins. Of course, it doesn't happen automatically; it takes some coaching from the teacher. Modeling proper small-group discussion is paramount to the success of this strategy. Discussions—in whole classes or in small groups—require detailed instructions. Once this is done, though, students should be able to engage one another with little assistance from the teacher.

First-year teacher Kelly Dillon quickly figured out the value of this strategy. Dillon used a student-centered approach for much of her class. The discussion strategy she implemented is based on Matt Copeland's *Socratic Circles* (2005). It employs a dual circle, in which the inside group debates a subject, while the outside group monitors and prepares additional points and counterpoints. According to Dillon, "I always knew I valued student-led discussion. It is a vehicle for critical and collaborative thinking, and it allows students to have a voice (literally) in the curriculum, which can so easily be co-opted by standards and district requirements." Best of all, Dillon learned in her first year what it took me more than 16 years to stumble upon—her students often learn more from one another than from their teachers. "The point is this: I have learned this year that less is more. The less I do to prepare 'lessons' and the more I leave the trajectory of the class up to students, the more they learn."

To further underscore this strategy, think back for a moment to the minilesson and discovery activity example I shared earlier. An entire 46-minute class period consisted of me sharing a list of literary terms and asking my students to learn about each one. There was a question-and-answer session that lasted about one minute and a single two-minute interruption when I shared a video. Closing the activity, I told students we'd apply what they learned to year-long projects, which we would discuss further the following day. All told, I talked for a total of approximately 6 of our 46 minutes together. That means my students heard my voice for about 13 percent of our class time. The remaining 87 percent was all about them. One hundred percent of the students, though, mastered the learning outcome.

If you often use visual aids and ask students to write about them, stop talking or say less than usual. This may take a methodical effort. When I realized that I droned on relentlessly (you'll know you do if you scan the room and only one or two students are looking at you), I began a strange practice of timing myself. I would stroll around the classroom with a stopwatch in hand and literally time how many minutes I was talking without interruption. My original goal was to never talk for more than three minutes at a time. This, of course, was unrealistic in a traditional classroom, because lecturing was part of my routine; it was one of my many crutches. When I shifted to a results-only style, I eliminated the stopwatch, as the need to talk decreased daily. Using the year-long project (Strategy 1) as a daily activity and transitioning to a workshop setting (Strategy 4), I found that the students were working together to meet our objectives, and I became more of a coach than a traditional stand-and-deliver teacher.

Many days require no direct instruction at all, whereas others may include a five-minute minilesson that is built around a slide show or brief video. These minilessons are designed to deliver a message that gets students comparing, summarizing, analyzing, and collaborating in order to apply the objective back to the year-long project, a separate project, or a single in-class activity. The idea here is to get complete involvement from students for most of the class. Educators and authors Pérsida and William Himmele call activities that facilitate complete student involvement Total Participation Techniques—tools "that allow for all students to demonstrate, at the same time, active participation and cognitive engagement in the topic being studied" (2011, p. 7). Let me illustrate with an example of my own. In Chapter 2, I briefly discussed

our year-long diary writing project, for which students create a character and place him or her in a specific time in history. The student tells a
story from that character's point of view. I can begin a class by saying,
"Let's spend today working on our diary project," and students can
easily fill a large block of time writing, sharing, or researching the time
period about which they're writing.

Another minilesson involves sharing model entries that I write for
my own diary project. Just as reading along with students is a key piece
of the Reading All Year project, I write with my students, too, as it's
important for them to see that I am as invested as they are. Periodically,
I post samples of my own writing to our classroom website, and I point
students to these entries while we're using computers. I could just as
easily show the diary entry on our interactive whiteboard, but I would
likely lose some of the audience. Using the computer to have students
read the sample diary entry is my own version of the Himmeles' Total
Participation Techniques. As all students read, I will say a few things
about the writing and what motivated me to compose certain sentences.
Then I'll stop talking. Almost immediately, hands will go up and students
will ask specific questions. Sometimes I answer; other times, I ask them
to get the opinion of a classmate. With Forget's research in mind, I want
students to discuss the material, rather than listen to me talk about it.

Yet another example of a diary project minilesson that requires virtually no direct instruction is one on improving diction. I show students
a video slideshow I created with sentences that contain weak verbs and
adjectives. The presentation suggests replacement words to strengthen
each sentence. Again, I say nothing; the video speaks for itself. The only
talking I do is to pose a crucial question: "Now that you've seen how
sentences can be improved with a few choice words, can you improve
your own writing like this?" I barely finish the question before students
race off to their diary entries and begin replacing weak verbs and adjectives with stronger ones. If we have computers, then I'll circulate and
spark more student discussion with simple statements and questions.

"I see Sarah found a nice website that suggests strong words," I'll announce. With no further direction, students will scurry over to Sarah and look over her shoulder or shout across the room, asking her to share the address of the website. "I wonder if there are similar vocabulary sites we could use," I say to no one in particular. A minute later, five students have located different online word applications and are sharing them with the class. This is the sort of good chaos that occurs daily in a results-only classroom. Rather than fearing a loss of control, you should embrace this chaos, because powerful learning takes place in moments such as these. Sure, you may occasionally have to ask for voices to be lowered, and sometimes students may drift away from the assignment to other inviting places on the Internet, but this isn't reason enough to eliminate the good chaos of a ROLE. Be vigilant, giving gentle reminders about respecting the freedom provided in the results-only classroom, and, eventually, all unwanted distractions will dissipate.

Remember, the key to successful chaos is in your own silence. When you find yourself talking for an extended period of time, make yourself talk less.

Strategy 3: Build Choice into All Activities

By now you know that a ROLE is built on autonomy. We want our students to learn; how they get there is secondary, but it will be much easier for them to get there if they choose their own paths. With this in mind, try to build choice into all your in-class activities. Incorporating choice is easy, as long as you create a variety of opportunities for students to demonstrate learning. If the activity includes writing, give students the choice of placing their prose in a journal or on a blog. For parts of speech, have students choose one and teach it to the class any way they know how—a song, poem, dance, or podcast, to name a few. If there are 10 math problems to complete, have small-group members each pick three or four. Then ask them to teach their solutions to another group. For a science project on the solar system, share minilessons that include videos on planets, moons, the sun, and anything else the unit requires. Then tell your students to show off what they've learned with a presentation, using any of the tools at their fingertips. When you let them decide how to do it, you will be amazed at how eager even your most reluctant learners are to share knowledge.

In an education system driven by high-stakes testing, we've been conditioned to teach to the test. Keep in mind that a results-only classroom will prepare your students to do well on a standardized test, and at the same time teach them lessons that extend far beyond state standards. The key is to provide choices in how they learn the standards. (See Chapter 8 for how students in a ROLE outperform their traditional classroom peers on standardized tests.)

Let's assume I have numerous reading standards that I need students to meet. In my class, we often use newspapers, but we do far more than just examine articles or learn about journalism. I want my students to learn about nonfiction and journalism, and I want them to be critical thinkers. With that in mind, the newspaper activities are created independent of state standards. Throughout the year, students learn to browse, preview, question, share, and employ a myriad of reading strategies. Newspaper days are one-day, in-class activity days. They rarely carry over to another class day, but students may connect the many lessons from these days to a project on which they are working. The activities associated with these lessons ultimately meet state-mandated standards and prepare students for an achievement test, but they aren't narrowly geared directly to the test. When projects and activities are built for learning, they typically hit the standards in one way or another. They create powerful learning opportunities and keep students engaged with the autonomy that a ROLE provides.

We meet many standards in this one-class period, which will be reinforced weekly with the use of newspapers. Here is a short list of

Grade 7 and 8 standards that can easily be met in one class, using a ROLE activity that involves student autonomy:

1. Cite several pieces of textual evidence to support analysis of what the text says explicitly as well as inferences drawn from the text.

2. Determine the meaning of words and phrases as they are used in the text.

3. Determine an author's point of view or purpose in a text and analyze how the author acknowledges and responds to conflicting evidence or viewpoints.

4. Analyze a case in which two or more texts provide conflicting information on the same topic, and identify where the texts disagree on matters of fact or interpretation.

In years past, when I taught to the test, I would have assigned an article from the newspaper and given students a fill-in-the-blank worksheet to meet these standards. The worksheet contained items such as "What is the main idea?" and "Supply two details from the story to support the main idea." Of course, the worksheet gave most of the information, so there was little thinking involved, and there was no autonomy or collaboration of any kind.

In a results-only classroom, I meet the standards and their benchmarks with much more student-centered activities. Students demonstrate mastery in one day, completing what I call Create-a-Question. Each student spends three to five minutes browsing the newspaper, looking for an interesting news story. I remind them of an earlier lesson on distinguishing news from commentary (i.e., fact from opinion). The browsing immediately pulls students into the activity because it's very tactile, and they know they have the freedom to choose something of interest to them personally. When they finish, I display very specific instructions on the interactive whiteboard. The gist of the activity is for students to read the news article they've selected, play teacher for a day, and create their own questions.

"Imagine you are assigning your news article to me," I say. "You want to challenge me with probing, short answer questions about the main idea, setting, vocabulary, point of view, or other things in the article you feel are important." I remind them of the essential questions—*who, what, when, where, why, how*—which we reviewed earlier in the year. These interrogatives will help them form their questions. This is one of the most successful individual activities we complete all year, although it can certainly be done in groups if the students choose to work cooperatively. They may prefer to share an article and create questions together. In a ROLE, this is always acceptable.

Create-a-Question not only exemplifies a ROLE activity that embraces choice but also underscores how easy it is to evaluate benchmarks through simple observation. I don't need to collect or grade anything because I read over my students' shoulders or listen in as they discuss among their groups. I provide verbal feedback to every student, and I can type brief comments into our online grade book if I feel it's necessary. I'll share more on the effectiveness and ease of this type of feedback in Chapters 5 and 6. It's worth noting here, though, that this is a move away from grading. The transition from points, percentages, and letter grades to feedback is integral to the successful move from traditional teaching to results-only learning.

Eliminate grades? Is this even possible? Remember first-year teacher Kelly Dillon and her use of Socratic seminars to engage students? (One student, she reports, even asked a guidance counselor to postpone a meeting because he didn't want to miss a seminar.) In spite of her students' enthusiasm, it didn't take Dillon long to learn that grades diminished the effectiveness of the seminars. "The mistake we were making was that we graded the discussions," Dillon says. "How else are we supposed to motivate kids to participate if not by assigning points? When I realized my mistake, a whole new world of teaching and learning opened up before my eyes. By removing the grade as an incentive, I allowed students to relax and focus on learning. The irony is that students aren't motivated by points to prepare but rather by the fact that coming unprepared means they can't participate in the inner circle of the seminar." This is one example of the amazing impact that student choice and the elimination of grades have on learning and how this approach will forever change teaching and learning in your class.

Strategy 4: Convert to a Workshop Setting

Since converting my classroom to a ROLE, I toyed with the idea of giving it a cool name that uses the word *workshop.* I eventually dropped that idea since I already use the word periodically in association with other projects, such as Readers' Workshop, Writers' Workshop, Poets' Workshop, and others. Honestly, I probably use the word too much. I like it, though, because I consider my class to be more of a workshop than a traditional classroom. The physical space of my classroom has desks scattered about in pods of four or five. Bookcases line the walls, and student work is hung in no particular order from one corner to the next. Beanbag chairs are scattered haphazardly, providing comfort for students during reading or small-group collaboration. Five computers are nestled snugly against one wall (I'm always trying to get more), and one or two carts occupy whatever space they can, holding student notebooks, paperbacks, or art supplies that are available for projects.

On many days, passersby peek in to see what the excitement is all about. They might observe five students at computers updating their reading plans or adding annotations to our classroom Diigo website, while two or three others help organize our vast library. Four more students might be whispering about books they're reading, while several others lounge in beanbags with their paperbacks, Kindles, or iPods, pencils in hand, ready to reflect on their stories. If John Dewey traveled through time and walked into our room, he probably wouldn't recognize it as a typical class, but I bet he'd like it nonetheless. Although it's unrealistic to believe this sort of chaotic activity can take place every day, creating a workshop environment is imperative to the success of a results-only classroom.

When educators Angela Maiers and Amy Sandvold (2011) talk about learning clubs, they are referring to groups of students that operate in a workshop setting. Maiers and Sandvold identify four key parts of successful learning clubs, which also align with the workshop components of a ROLE. They are interdependence (collaboration), authenticity (engaging in cross-curricular thinking), digitally driven learning (technology use), and independence (choice in how and what to study). To create an efficient workshop, it's important for students to adapt to these components, even if they don't understand the terms themselves. From the first day of school, students in a results-only classroom are taught these elements. We start in small groups and discuss proper collaboration. We begin using computers right away; students set up classroom websites, which they'll use all year to demonstrate learning. We begin our Reading All Year project during the first week; students learn the value of choice as they develop their own reading plans for the year. I may never use the terms *interdependence* or *cross-curricular thinking*, but the ideas they represent are present all year in a Results Only Learning Environment.

Like other ROLE strategies, shifting your current classroom environment to a workshop setting may be difficult at first. The control you're used to maintaining will have to dissipate. This isn't easy; so many traditionalists and bureaucrats, who portray themselves as education experts, perpetuate the idea that a silent, almost churchlike atmosphere is a compulsory part of a quality education. One such self-portrayed expert, Robert Earl, a private contractor who works primarily in corporate project management, claims that "silence in class is an all-too-rare phenomenon. If the teacher isn't talking or an instructional video isn't playing, there's likely to be the incessant talking of students among themselves. All in all, there is lots of *Sturm and Drang*, not enough contemplative thinking and learning" (2012, para. 10). This *Sturm* and *Drang*, which can be translated loosely as "storm" and "urge," is exactly the sort of environmental attribute that makes a ROLE's workshop setting successful. Sadly, people such as Earl, who have never worked as classroom teachers, send the wrong message to a wide audience—including parents and school administrators—suggesting that these interactions are damaging education. For a results-only classroom to succeed, the silence has to be interrupted, and teachers must change their strategies. "Stop managing and controlling them," says nationally recognized teacher and education writer Pernille Ripp. "You control animals and manage tasks, not children. How about guiding or leading them instead?" (2011b, para. 9)

I started the transition to a workshop setting a few years ago. Rows of desks turned into pods. Although rearranging desks is fairly simple, it can be quite daunting if you've lived in the row world your entire teaching career. At first, be careful to separate children you believe may cause problems. As the year goes on, this will be less of an issue because once you've thoroughly fanned your students' intrinsic motivation and thrown out the worksheets and lectures, they will forget about being disruptive (I'll elaborate on this in Chapter 9). The desired "good chaos" will begin to evolve in these cooperative groups as students discuss activities and projects in which they are engaged. Maiers and Sandvold's learning club elements—interdependence, authenticity, and digitally driven learning—will make learning fun and disruption passé.

In addition to this, a workshop setting embraces what can be the traditional teacher's worst nightmare—movement. During the my-way-or-the-highway days, the expectation was that students would remain glued to their seats. I might have literally glued them down if I could have gotten away with it. A static classroom, in which only the teacher moves, is the epitome of a controlled environment. The theory is that if students aren't moving, then there will be no problems. Of course, this control is merely an illusion. Most bored students eventually become unruly and find a way to disrupt the class, even if they decide to remain seated. In a ROLE, there's no reason to fear movement because students only move with a purpose. This is part of the intrinsic motivation that is coached from the beginning of the year and the wonderful gift of freedom that the workshop setting provides. If you teach students that autonomy has to be respected, then they will respect it, so let them move. Paul Anderson, the 2011 Montana Teacher of the Year, has created a workshop setting that is filled with good chaos. "If you were to come in, you would find kids reading, watching videos . . . doing special activities, trying to solve challenges, working together, or working alone" (Anderson, 2012). Allowing students to get up for a tissue, sharpen a pencil, talk about a project with peers in a different group, or simply stretch their legs is the sort of chaos that is completely acceptable in a workshop atmosphere.

Don't forget, though, that the teacher is a critical part of the workshop. As a teacher, you need to be more than a leader. You need to be a facilitator, coach, questioner, and partner. Workshops will fail if the facilitator sits back and watches or, worse, roams around and does nothing more than hover over the participants. What I love most about the workshop setting in a results-only classroom is the freedom I have to build rapport with my students. I glide around the room while students are working on anything from individual activities to one whole-class project. I'm much more than an observer, though. If a student is updating a reading plan, then I stop to look in and ask about a particular title or share my feelings on the book, if I've read it. If a book chat is taking place in another group, then I'll sit in an open seat and be an active participant, eliciting input from each group member in an unobtrusive way. (Participation shouldn't look like assessment or a search for accountability.)

"Oh, I nearly cried when Rue was dying," I might say about Suzanne Collins's *The Hunger Games.* "I don't think I've ever read such a powerful scene. How did you react to the way Collins handled Rue's death, Emily?" The students see me as a visitor to their book chat, rather than as a teacher, interested only in testing their reading comprehension. Emily's response to my simple question is her way of giving me invaluable feedback about her understanding of and connection to the story. I learn a lot about Emily and her peers from this simple discussion, and I don't need to quiz them or have them complete book summaries.

When I leave that chat, I might stop by students who are organizing books and ask their opinions about changing our system. "I've been thinking about making each shelf a different genre," I'll suggest. "What do you think?" Not only am I observing the organization and cooperative skills required in their task, I'm also gaining trust by asking for their opinions—something that plays far too small a role in today's classrooms.

To have successful chaos, it's important to let some things happen that a traditional classroom teacher would never allow. This might even mean sometimes looking the other way and pretending not to notice what students are doing. This may seem impossible for the traditionalist who is always sweating the small stuff. There will be much more on rules and consequences later in this book; for now, let's consider some unnecessary rules that hinder a workshop setting, such as one that disallows food or drink in the classroom. Imagine any workshop you've ever attended. You sit and listen to a facilitator while sipping on hot coffee, tea, or a cold bottle of water.

Although I wouldn't necessarily recommend inviting your students to bring lattes to class (this could be fun in some cases, though), what's the harm in letting students have bottled water in your room? Sure, this may not work in a computer lab, but for now, let's think about a standard classroom, minus the technological gadgets. Would you be breaking a school rule if you allowed your students to have water? Maybe. So why not look the other way? My students break lots of rules that I deem relatively insignificant but make our workshop setting function more effectively. I don't tell them that it's okay to break school rules. When they ask, I simply say, "The school policy is no food or drink." Quizzical looks are followed by "Okay, does that mean I can't bring my water bottle?" I smile and repeat the prior refrain: "School policy says no food or drink." This may continue for a couple of minutes before another student, slightly more intuitive than her friend, pipes in with, "He doesn't care, but he can't tell you that." I just smile and shrug my shoulders, and we move on. Let me tell you, since I started allowing water in my room, there has not been a single spill. Remember, students respect the gift of autonomy.

Strategy 5: Integrate Technology

As you've already seen, technology is a huge part of the results-only classroom. Students engage in activities and projects more efficiently when using the Internet, and websites provide a powerful platform for creating two-way narrative feedback. I realize there are still many school districts that are short on computers, which makes relying on them all the more difficult. However, in a Race-to-the-Top, Common-Core-State-Standards world, there is a heavy emphasis on technology integration, so government funding is available in many cases. In addition, as mobile technology continues to develop, unit prices are decreasing and tools are becoming more affordable to even poorer school districts. What makes technology integration easiest, though, is the Bring Your Own Device movement. Nearly one-fourth of students ages 12–17 have a smartphone, and for students who are 14–17 years old, that number increases to 31 percent (Lenhart, 2012). Sadly, too many school districts are missing out on a remarkable learning opportunity by mandating that cell phones remain in lockers or turned off during the school day.

If you have access to computers, outdated cell phone policies won't hurt you as much. However, convincing administrators to abandon the rules against mobile devices makes technology integration much easier. "We're well into the 21st century, and it's time for schools to encourage educators to start using methods that will prepare students for their future rather than relying on the comfortable policies and methods of the past. . . . It is incumbent upon educators to empower students to be independent and responsible learners who can self-monitor and discover the optimal conditions to learn and create" (Nielsen, 2012, para. 3, 18). In a Results Only Learning Environment, students use smartphones and other mobile learning devices such as iPods, Kindles, and Nooks, on a daily basis. The key is to coach students early and often about appropriate use. Remember that breaking a few well-chosen rules is typically more helpful than harmful to a ROLE. The no-cell-phone policy is a bad rule that is certainly worth breaking. I tell my students that although the school policy mandates that cell phones and other mobile devices must be put away, we will use them for learning. I am always the squeaky wheel at my school, trumpeting the value of cell phones and other mobile devices for learning.

In our workshop setting, students use computers and mobile devices to read, write, and review my narrative feedback. They even post to our classroom blog, their private individual web pages (which are hosted on our classroom website), and our private social book-marking site using smartphones, iPods, and tablets. Some students rate, review, and share books on the social networking site Goodreads, and others create interactive web-based posters that contain outside article links, their own written content, and embedded YouTube videos, which can then be shared with peers with one click or embedded on our classroom blog. Not only do these devices and applications create autonomy and encourage intrinsic motivation, they also provide a platform for sharing.

The days of physical hard copies in education are over. Collecting handwritten essays and worksheets is an archaic practice that has no place in the 21st century Results Only Learning Environment. As a language arts teacher, I want my students to respond to fiction and nonfiction. I want them to conduct research and cite sources. However, I'd never ask them to use a physical encyclopedia or write facts on index cards. Instead, students could find anything they need on Google Scholar, Wikipedia, Fact Monster, About.com, or a myriad of other online resources. They can share their information via Diigo, Evernote, Google Docs, Facebook, Twitter, or some other website, making peer and teacher review and feedback immediate.

Individual and collaborative activities and projects flow through the web tools and applications we use. Of course, effective technology integration means learning how to use a wide array of applications and taking the time to teach them to students. This may seem daunting, but there is plenty of help just a mouse click away. Websites such as FreeTech4Teachers.com, Learnitin5.com, and MakeUseOf.com—to name a few—are powerful resources that provide easy how-to videos and content for learning web tools. Incorporate a five-minute lesson a few times a month on a new web tool and how to apply it to learning, and your students will soon have their own digital toolkit, which they can then use to demonstrate mastery learning. This is results-only learning. The teacher asks for a result—a learning outcome—and provides numerous paths that students can take to demonstrate understanding. As the school year progresses, students will become more efficient at locating their own web tools. Soon, they may even teach you something new about technology, and that isn't a bad thing.

Results-only learning may be considered a major reform, but it really boils down to these five strategies:

1. Incorporate the year-long project.
2. Talk less.
3. Build choice into all activities.
4. Convert to a workshop setting.
5. Integrate technology.

The strategies may look simple here in black and white, but the implementation takes a great amount of thought and conviction. Follow these steps, though, and be persistent. You'll soon find yourself immersed in a flourishing Results Only Learning Environment.

5

Moving from Grades to Feedback: Say It, Write It, Listen to It

I always thought feedback would help me more than grades would. I would get a test back with a percentage, but I never knew what I was doing wrong. There would be circles and Xs all over my paper that I couldn't make sense of. It all seemed like a big tic-tac-toe game to me. Teachers never left comments. They just expected me to know why something was circled. I like to know what I did wrong, and I like to know what I did right. Knowing where you excelled helps you improve. You know the areas that you need some work on and the areas that you don't have to focus on. Numbers just put stress on students. You get a low grade, and you're stressing to get it back up. You get a high grade, and you are stressing to keep it up. Either way, the numbers and grades cause a huge amount of stress for students. You quickly cram information into your head before a test. Once the test is over, you forget it all. If you are too busy trying to get the grade you want, you won't learn. But if you are constantly receiving feedback on how to improve, you will learn. If teachers just lecture, give tests, and move on, they aren't trying to make sure you completely understand the information. These teachers just want you to understand things enough to pass a state administered test. Feedback can help you improve to become better than you are. This is why I believe feedback is better than receiving grades.
—Mikayla Colston, 8th grade ROLE student

Imagine how many people could have gone to college, landed a better job, or even been elected president if they had gotten higher grades during their K–12 years. When I was in school, sitting among rows of desks, and wondering how the lectures I was hearing would matter in the real world, I somehow managed to make average grades. The only reason I was admitted to the small liberal arts college I attended was because my sister went there, and I got a recommendation from one of the school's most successful students. As anyone can infer, I was lucky. Most students don't have this sort of good fortune, and in our current broken system, they need above-average grades to get into good colleges. To put a finer point on this, students' futures, in many ways, depend on their teachers. They show up, turn in their worksheets, take multiple-choice tests, and hope their teachers like them enough to give them high grades, because those grades mean everything to their academic future.

A Results Only Learning Environment takes the emphasis off grades and puts it squarely on learning. Throughout this book, I've discussed how difficult the transition from traditional teaching to ROLE-style teaching can be, and giving up grades is certainly not easy. For many years, I could never have imagined an education world without grades. Now there is no realistic possibility of ever returning to the practice of placing points, percentages, and letters on my students' work. When I tell colleagues and friends that I don't grade, they are perplexed. Eyebrows furrow instantly, and the question is always the same, no matter who is asking: "How does that work?" This simple query is followed in most cases by a more specific question: "How do you judge their work? What do parents say?" Of course, I also often hear, "How does your principal feel about that?" To most people, school without grades is sort of like a car without wheels; it just doesn't make sense. Education researcher Alfie Kohn, however, brings the matter into focus:

If we begin with a desire to assess more often, or to produce more data, or to improve the consistency of our grading, then certain prescriptions will follow. If, however, our point of departure is the desire for students to understand ideas from the inside out, or to get a kick out of playing with words and numbers, or to be in charge of their own learning, then we may come to see grading as a huge, noisy, fuel-guzzling, smoke-belching machine that constantly requires repairs and new parts, when what we should be doing is pulling the plug. (Kohn, 2011, p. 32)

So, in this chapter, I'll first examine how grades affect students. Then I'll show you, as Kohn says, how to pull the plug on them and—perhaps most important—what to replace them with.

Why Do We Grade?

Whether it's intentional or preconditioned, most teachers think of grades as measuring sticks. Students become labeled by a letter. A counselor may say, "He's a *C* student in math but a *B* student in social studies." A parent asks, "How did you do on your science project, honey?" The child answers, "Oh, I got a *B+*." Most parents will respond with a simple "Oh, that's great," unless that student has previously been labeled as an *A* student. If that is the case, then the parent may angrily shout, "Well, that's not good enough! You know we expect nothing less than *A*s from you." Unfortunately, a student who performed well above average, at least according to traditional grading scales, on what may have been a very difficult project, is attacked because she's less than perfect in her parents' eyes. This may represent a different kind of problem, but at least on the surface, the issue is about grades.

If these hypothetical scenarios are accurate, then why do we continue to grade? Why do teachers feel obligated to collect assignments and attach points, percentages, or letters to them? A quiz has 20 questions, so it has to be worth 20 points, unless 20 points do not put enough weight on the quiz, in which case the teacher may double the value to

40. A health essay on the deleterious effects of cigarettes on the body is randomly assigned a value of 50 points. Where does this number originate? Why isn't the paper worth 100 or even 1,000 points? More perplexing is the 5-point bell work, formerly one of my personal favorites: complete a workbook page in 10 minutes and receive 5 points. This and similar brief activities effectively provide participation points—another crutch that many teachers primarily use as a classroom management tool. If grades are nothing more than tools for measuring performance, then we must wonder what 5-point bell work assignments or participation points are actually measuring.

Do we really want to grade participation? Shouldn't the real goal be to have students learn? If the latter is true and we measure learning with grades, then taking points from a student because she does not speak during a discussion or raise her hand at least once a week is detrimental to the actual goal; the zero only punishes her. Furthermore, if something such as participation is lumped in with more substantive activities toward an overall grade and if grades are, in fact, measuring sticks, then is a nonparticipating student really only average if he or she gets a *C* in a marking period? One might argue that including participation in grading creates a subjective aspect. However, upon closer examination, it is logical to say that grading, in general, is subjective.

"Even the score on a math test is largely a reflection of how the test was written: what skills the teacher decided to assess, what kinds of questions happened to be left out, and how many points each section was 'worth'" (Kohn, 2000, p. 41). In fact, formal assessments, whether purposely or inadvertently, are routinely manipulated by teachers to generate a particular outcome. Study guides ask for rote memorization of skills and concepts taught throughout a learning unit, and rubrics are nothing more than subjective checklists students can use to create what they believe the teacher wants to see. Weighting assignments punishes students who are perceived as lazy and rewards those considered to be hard-working. All these tools and methods affect grades. None is objective, though, and not a single one provides meaningful feedback about learning.

Replace Grades with Feedback

Let's assume that the most important goal of any teacher is for students to learn. Taking this a step further, I think we can agree that learning is the goal of education in general. If this is absolute, and if grades only pass judgment, then we have to at least consider they may be a useless part of learning. To illustrate, let's assume a student receives a *B+* on her science project. Does she learn anything from the *B+*? Perhaps she knows that this is above average, based on all she's learned about grades, so she feels that she has done well. Can she, though, apply the *B+* back to any of the project's learning outcomes? At this point, skeptics will contend that a rubric is used to arrive at the *B+*. Still, do we assume that students understand objectives or that they connect a number or letter grade back to a rubric? I could spend pages on the subjectivity and lack of fairness of rubrics, most of which do not consider a student's point of view of the activity.

Others suggest that a comment accompanying the grade is, in effect, the same as narrative feedback. This is not the case, though, according to researcher Dylan Wiliam. After 25 years studying assessments, Wiliam concludes that adding comments to grades does not improve those grades (2011). In fact, he concludes that adding diagnostic comments to scores or grades is a waste of time. In a previous study, Wiliam and some colleagues found that "Students given marks are likely to see it as a way to compare themselves with others; those given only comments see it as helping them to improve. The latter group outperforms the former" (Black et al., 2004, p. 18). Although the research supporting narrative feedback is exhaustive, the work of Wiliam and his colleagues is most noteworthy and should give any educator pause before assigning points, percentages, or letters to an activity or a project.

As long as we're considering the possibility that letter grades are deleterious to learning, we need to also consider what might fill the gap and be a good replacement. I would argue that narrative feedback is one of the strongest contenders for that slot. Feedback is not new. Researchers have examined narrative feedback for decades. "Feedback is information with which a learner can confirm, add to, overwrite, tune, or restructure information in memory, whether that information is domain knowledge, meta-cognitive knowledge, beliefs about self and tasks, or cognitive tactics and strategies" (Winne & Butler, 1994, p. 5740). Even though feedback has been around for many years, it usually accompanies grades and is poorly written. Other researchers understand this: "Feedback is among the most critical influences on student learning. A major aim of the educative process is to assist in identifying these gaps ('How am I going?' relative to 'Where am I going?') and to provide remediation in the form of alternative or other steps ('Where to next?')" (Hattie & Timperly, 2007, p. 102). This connection between where students are headed and how to get them there is where meaningful narrative feedback comes in—feedback that is far more than a smiley face sticker, a check mark, or a note that simply says "good job."

To thoroughly understand the effect of feedback in place of number or letter grades, let's begin by considering one large activity or project you might assign. If your class has 1,000 points per grading period, then this project or assignment might comprise 200 of those points, or 20 percent of the final grade. (It took me many years to realize, when it comes to understanding achievement, how arbitrary and illogical these weights are.) Keep in mind that the most important goal of the activity is learning, so you're going to eliminate any points, percentages, or letters you previously attached to the assignment. Instead, you'll get feedback from your students about the project, and you'll provide ongoing narrative feedback both during the project and after the work is completed. A student's response is also feedback—the kind that helps the teacher provide follow-up lessons, which allow for mastery (Barnes, 2011). What makes this system so successful is that it leaves final action in the hands of the students, providing them with legitimate opportunities for learning. Since feedback is narrative, a teacher can summarize what has been accomplished, explain exactly what a student needs to do to demonstrate he or she has met an objective, redirect the student to further instruction, and request resubmission of the activity or project when it's been reworked. I call this system of feedback SE2R.

SE2R: Summarize, Explain, Redirect, Resubmit

Effective narrative feedback should always *summarize* and *explain* what a student has accomplished, based on the activity or project guidelines. If the learning outcome is mastered, then the feedback will end with these two components of the SE2R system. If further learning is required, then the student will be *redirected* to prior instruction and then *resubmit* the work for teacher evaluation. Although some educators might question the effectiveness of narrative feedback, the SE2R system is far less subjective than placing a number or letter on a student's work. The key to successful feedback is remaining as objective as possible. It's okay to tell a child that her work is "nicely done" but only after a detailed summary and explanation have been provided.

The SE2R feedback in Figure 5.1 is based on a writing activity. Students need to post a how-to article on our classroom blog, which is located at www.KidBlog.com. Students are instructed to review their completed posts and replace weak words with stronger ones, drawing on an in-class presentation about "words that pop." Before they publish their final posts, students highlight the "words that pop" in a color of their choice (more autonomy). Commas should also be placed after introductory elements and highlighted, drawing on a separate in-class lesson. The SE2R example in Figure 5.1 may look like a lot of writing for one student, but experience will help you limit your words. Keep in mind that many students will master the activity on the first attempt, eliminating the need for redirection and a request for resubmission. Finally, this labeling format (i.e., Summarize, Explain, Redirect, Resubmit) is only used to illustrate how the SE2R system works. Using SE2R labels is a choice for individual teachers to make. It may be especially effective for elementary students, but some teachers of older students may also prefer to label their narrative feedback, rather than write in sentence or paragraph form.

5.1 | Sample Student Feedback Using the SE2R System

Summarize: You have completed a how-to article and posted it to KidBlog. You highlighted words in the post in order to demonstrate understanding of the "Words that Pop" presentation.

Explain: The highlighted words are not words that make the writing "pop." Also, we reviewed how to use commas after introductory words and phrases, yet you haven't placed any commas by these words. For example, *first*, *next*, and *then* are all introductory words that should be followed by a comma.

Redirect: You should review the presentation on strong adjectives and verbs, linked under RAY on www.barnesclass.com. Then return to your how-to blog and improve it, based on the presentation. Also, add the commas where needed.

Resubmit: When this is done, please go to the "Write to Mr. Barnes" section on our classroom website and tell me that you have resubmitted this activity.

Colleagues often wonder where I find time to provide feedback to more than one hundred students each year. Admittedly, it's not easy. I spend more time providing feedback than I spend on anything else. Using the SE2R approach streamlines and simplifies the process, though. Regardless of what activity or project we're working on, I begin by telling students what they've done. This may sound inconsequential, but many students complete tasks aimlessly and never realize what they've actually accomplished. Further explanation of what was done and how it does or doesn't meet learning outcomes or follow a specific set of guidelines is critical to the learning process. If something is missed, students are redirected to a specific lesson, presentation, or model so learning can be reemphasized. Sometimes, redirection can be as simple as "see me for clarification." When redirection is given, students are always asked to resubmit the activity or project for further evaluation. When we discuss this process in class, it is called the circle of learning—the circle is only complete when mastery learning takes place.

Feedback in Action

The examples of narrative feedback that follow illustrate just how much this kind of feedback impacts learning and how it effectively replaces grades. Furthermore, it underscores some of the most recent research by leading authorities in education. "If feedback is directed at the right level, it can assist students to comprehend, engage, or develop effective strategies to process the information intended to be learned" (Hattie & Timperly, 2007, p. 104). Comprehension, engagement, and development of strategies are evident in the examples below. Note that for most activities, narrative feedback begins with a verbal exchange between teacher and student. After the teacher evaluates an activity and supplies written narrative feedback, the student can make changes and resubmit the activity. Each of the following examples briefly outlines the activity or project and shares real feedback that was given for students of varying ability levels.

Activity 1: Book Commercial

This is a brief oral presentation that includes a short summary of a book, a reading from the book (that is selected by the student), and a personal opinion about the book. Commercials are typically one to two minutes in length, but a significant amount of preparation, including reading the whole book, goes into the presentation, making it a substantial project.

Billy: A student who read below grade level, Billy was one of my toughest students, and he openly admitted he did not like to read. He completed four books in a semester, which was well below our goal, but it was four more than he'd ever read on his own prior to joining our class. Before he delivered his commercial, we discussed his book—by Walter Dean Myers—which I had already read. He showed me the selection he wanted to share, which was not too long and included moments of suspense that most students would enjoy. After Billy presented his book commercial to the class, I left the following feedback on our web-based grade book: "I like the reading selection as it's suspenseful, but you need to practice it and read it with more enthusiasm; good summary information, but I'm still not sure how much you've read, based on the details you provide. I like the endorsement, especially how you mention the movie scenes."

Notice that the SE2R is mixed throughout the brief feedback. I explained that Billy read a suspenseful selection and offered a solid general summary, but one that was devoid of detail. The redirection was given to the entire class; I explained that information about book commercials could be found on our classroom website and that all students should review it. I also redirected Billy to practice while he was reading my written feedback. Brief verbal comments, given as students read written ones, often prove to be an effective means of emphasizing part of the written narrative. Billy's revised book commercial added necessary details to the summary, indicating better comprehension. Our conversation prior to the commercial was a simple one that took place during a brief sidebar, while students prepared commercial notes at their seats: "Remember how your last commercial lacked good detail? Let's make sure this one offers enough details so I can tell you really understood the story." The casual nature of this 30-second conversation encouraged Billy to improve on something he did earlier and demonstrate that he had mastered a reading objective. His presentation was nearly perfect, and no points, percentages, or letters were necessary.

Camryn: A student who read at grade level, Camryn read more than many of her peers, but she gravitated to books that were often below her level. She liked to read for fun, and since a love of reading is the most important step to getting students to read, I didn't discourage her selections. She completed her first book commercial without much help from me. Our initial conversation was nothing more than me asking if she was ready and if she had prepared all the required parts of the commercial. She convinced me she was ready and well prepared. Here is the feedback I left after Camryn's first book commercial: "Thanks for reading a selection, but it sounds more like a synopsis of the book. I'm interested about the cat clans, but I don't hear much about them in your summary. Try to be a bit more detailed next time. I do like your specific endorsement of the book for cat lovers."

When we casually spoke about the feedback (this conversation took place in a computer lab, while students were typing blog posts), Camryn explained that she thought that reading the synopsis was okay. I realized that this was as much my fault as it was hers, because I assumed she knew what to do rather than ask her to show me her selection, like I did with Billy.

"This isn't a big deal," I told Camryn. "Just look for something different next time you deliver a book commercial. Try to captivate your audience with something that will make them want to read the book." This brief, casual chat is a critical piece of narrative feedback and can often be done without much thought. The power of such conversations on learning is evident, though. Here is the feedback I left Camryn on her next commercial: "You handle the selection well, and it's much better than the synopsis you read in your first book commercial. I like the way you explain it, and I like your honesty, calling it silly while adding that it is still a fun book to read. The endorsement seems to encourage your listeners to check out the book."

This feedback made it easy for Camryn to see that she had progressed and learned, as she clearly improved on the areas that were weak in her first book commercial. This written narrative feedback, coupled with our casual chats (two-way oral feedback), served her much better than a letter grade would have. In fact, if I had "punished" her with a *C* on her first commercial, then she may have withdrawn from the activity and put no further effort into another commercial.

Activity 2: Reflection Letter Blog Post

This is another key piece of our year-long reading project. The reflection letter gives students a chance to share summary information, which helps me evaluate reading comprehension, and it also serves as an outlet for personal connection and student evaluation of the books they're reading. The reflection letter is a valuable resource that students and I share throughout the year, and it provides powerful feedback both ways. Sometimes students write in a reading journal, and I can grab the journal and write a quick comment in it. Other times, I ask students to take their best recent letter and post it to the student blog on our classroom website. This more formal activity, which I ask them to complete in a week, helps students focus on their writing skills while they present their best reflection. The blog is also a place where other students can supply additional feedback. Therefore, this engaging activity helps students hone their reading and writing and use higher-level thinking to evaluate the work of their peers.

Marcus: A good reader who sometimes performed beneath his ability, Marcus was the type of student who could aggravate teachers. He was bright and a solid reader, but he would sometimes "mail in" activities, and I often found myself asking him for more. "You need to challenge yourself," I'd say. Ever the polite young man, Marcus would nod and promise to do better next time. Because I had built a good relationship with Marcus, I felt confident providing feedback that was direct and critical: "This is the exact opposite of what I taught in class about a mix of summary and personal connection. You've given all summary and no personal connection at all. Plus, you haven't proofread for basic errors as was emphasized in class. Please resubmit this reflection with more personal connection; mix your summary info with personal thoughts, as demonstrated in the models shown in class. I look forward to seeing your changes to this letter."

This feedback was based on a three-sentence reflection letter that offered only a brief summary of a novel. Marcus's cursory effort was also filled with the kind of fundamental errors that he typically didn't make, meaning he skipped the editing and revising part of the activity entirely. Notice the simplicity of the feedback, using the SE2R approach. I said what Marcus did and how he did it in a couple sentences. He was redirected to samples of well-written reflections I shared with the class, which he could easily locate on our classroom website. The last sentence of the feedback was a friendly way of requesting resubmission without sounding too demanding. Suggesting that I'd like to see a rewritten letter leaves the choice of rewriting to him. When Marcus made a second attempt at this specific reflection, it was clear he had followed my narrative feedback. Here is my response to his new reflection letter: "This letter is far better than what I've seen from you so far; you have mixed brief summary information with personal connection, which you completely missed the first time. I would still like to see you 'stretch' your writing, as your post is a bit underdeveloped; think about elaborating on your personal connections next time."

Jack: A student who read above grade level but had some anxiety issues and organization problems, Jack was a fascinating young man with a wonderful mind. He always chose science fiction or fantasy books and read voraciously. Jack had average writing skills and would contribute to class discussions only when he felt confident in his answers. A quiet and aloof student, Jack would never ask for assistance, even though he needed guidance to help him clear his thoughts, organize his activities, and budget his time. Jack did not submit the reflection letter blog activity by the original due date. (Of course, in a ROLE, due dates are really just guidelines, designed to help students budget their time.) Ironically, as I was evaluating the posts and supplying narrative feedback, Jack was working in my classroom after school—something he rarely did unless encouraged by his mother.

Jack was working on his reading plan, which was, as alluded to earlier, lacking in genres not called science fiction. As Jack browsed books and updated his online plan, I noticed he hadn't submitted a reflection letter, so I asked him about it. In his usual nervous way, he sort of shrugged and said, "I didn't know how to do it." It was late in the school year, so I knew this was Jack's way of saying he forgot or just ignored it, because he was working on other things he felt were more important. So I pressed him. "Come on," I said sternly, "that's a copout and you know it. I've seen plenty of good writing from you this year, and a reflection letter is one of the easiest forms of writing that we do. It's a little summary information mixed with your own feelings. Finish up that reading plan, and get this thing posted before you leave." And he did. My feedback to him was as follows: "This is a marvelous reflection letter—some of your best writing. This should help build your confidence, as you thought you couldn't do it and, with only minor support from me, you wrote one of the best letters I've read. The feeling you put into the letter, wondering why the tough boy would cry over something seemingly insignificant, is brilliant. I'm looking forward to your next reflection."

Of course, Jack also got instant verbal feedback that day, as I made sure to read his post while he was still in the room. I did this so I could praise his work without embarrassing him in front of his peers. It was a nice moment as I gave him a shocked look, threw up my arms, and said, "Seriously? You think you can't write a reflection letter? This is absolutely fantastic—one of the best ones I've read." In classic Jack fashion, he gave a tiny, wrinkled smile and said nothing. Thereafter, he seemed a bit more confident and his writing only got better. Imagine if I had simply given Jack a zero on this assignment because he didn't do it. This powerful moment of self-realization and real learning would never have happened.

Activity 3: Research Project

The yearly research unit has always been a labor of hate for me. When I taught 7th grade, students typically joined my class with very little experience with research. Maybe 10 percent of them understood the process and even fewer knew how to paraphrase or cite sources. In the past, we used index cards for notes and source citations, and students typed their outlines and papers in a Word document. The unit consisted of note card checks (5 points per card for 10–20 cards), outline checks (40 points with one chance to get it right), and a final research paper (100 points, with heavy deductions for misplaced commas and improperly punctuated citations). Even though I coached students along the way, their grades were final. It was not unusual for half of my students to fail the entire unit, which severely damaged their overall grade. Obviously, there wasn't much learning achieved. Each year, though, I continued in this manner, trying in vain to teach 100 frustrated 12-year-olds the entire research process in four weeks. Then I moved to a results-only learning style, and things improved markedly.

Reevaluating this nightmarish learning unit, I knew it had to change, so I applied ROLE concepts. First and foremost, autonomy and collaboration had to be added. Students worked in groups of two or three and chose their own topics—anything that fit what I called "Discovery Research," which meant mysterious or widely misunderstood events or processes, such as the sinking of the *Titanic,* forensic science, or ancient civilizations. The learning teams decided how to conduct the research, using only the minilessons that I provided as their guides. Some groups used books, others chose websites, and some even found amazing videos. Since traditional notes and a paper were still required in my district, I had to teach these components. Technology advances, however, helped me eliminate index cards and hard copies.

Research teams submitted all their work on the web using an interactive research tool that helped with source organization and easy transition of notes to outline and final report. Best of all, this system provided a marvelous platform for two-way communication between the research teams and me. The web research tool created independent online workspaces for each research team. Group members could communicate with one another, and I could leave feedback anytime, which the students received instantaneously. This is remarkably powerful. As students worked in our media center and library, I circulated to ask probing questions that guided their research, or I sat unobtrusively at my computer watching their projects evolve and leaving ongoing narrative feedback online. This proved to be the most successful research project I had until that point. The following example underscores the effectiveness of creating a research project on the Internet and using web-based narrative feedback.

DeWayne, Montel, and David: DeWayne and Montel were a bit more motivated to perform than David was. Although they all share similar skill levels, DeWayne is probably the strongest reader. As a group, they chose mysterious creatures as the topic of their research project. After a few minor formatting issues with source cards, which the team changed after verbal feedback from me, their struggles started with the outline. The web-based program we use allowed for easy conversion of notes into an outline, which could be a double-edged sword, as it also made it easy to ignore proper formatting. The team members were dropping all their notes under one heading, which made for a cumbersome outline.

In the past, I would have collected a hard-copy outline and scored it, based on a rubric. Each team member might have received 28/40 and moved on to writing the research paper. Their grades would have plummeted, and they would not have learned through change. However, within the redesigned ROLE-aligned format, they received a simple piece of narrative feedback that sparked interest in learning: "You have moved effective notes into the outline section of the Noodle Tools program. Continue building the outline, but consider which note cards belong under the various Roman numerals. For example, all of your notes from the cards labeled Bigfoot should go under one Roman numeral, say I. Notes from cards labeled Loch Ness Monster would go under a different Roman numeral, say II."

Since we started each day with students reading the feedback I'd left the day before, the students in this group read my comment about their outline and came to me to follow up. They thought all they had to do was drag the cards over to the first Roman numeral on the web-based outline. They didn't understand the purpose of the other Roman numerals. This gave me an opportunity to review the lesson on composing an outline while they made changes in front of me. A paper outline would have made this lesson impossible. In this case, the boys learned how to create an effective outline, which helped build a successful research paper. They mastered an important learning outcome, and they were not punished by poor grades.

Flattening the Traditional Bell Curve

You've probably noticed by now that the most powerful aspect of narrative feedback is the mastery learning it fosters. Students take redirection from the feedback, change the work product, and resubmit it to demonstrate mastery learning. This is, unequivocally, how teaching and learning should function. Because of the amazing learning that narrative feedback produces, report card grades in a Results Only

Learning Environment are typically much higher than those in a traditional classroom.

As I was being interviewed for a teaching job many years ago, I was asked what my current grade distribution looked like. The question struck me as very strange, although my answer was even more bizarre. "I'm not sure," I said, groping desperately for a reasonable response. "It's probably your typical bell curve." I'll never know what kind of answer they wanted, because I didn't get the job. As the years have passed and my teaching philosophy has changed, I've often thought back to that interview and that question about grades. Upon further consideration, I found myself aggravated that a school district would pose such a ridiculous question to a potential new employee. I'm appalled by the notion that school administrators judge students based on their placement on a geometrically shaped object. Even more disconcerting is the theory that grade distribution is in any way related to teaching and learning.

Still, I did supply the bell curve answer during the interview, and for most of my teaching career, I subscribed to the theory that a bell-shaped grade distribution made for a successful school year. It just seemed reasonable. University of Kentucky education professor Thomas Guskey explains this theory as one of the obstacles in the way of grading reform: "If scores on intelligence tests tend to resemble a normal bell-shaped curve—and intelligence is clearly related to achievement—then grade distributions should be similar" (Guskey, 2011, p. 18). However, as Guskey further explains, this reasoning is flawed. "The normal bell-shaped curve describes the distribution of randomly occurring events *when nothing intervenes*." In education, there are many interventions that affect randomly occurring events. For example, teachers and their subjectivity intervene daily, and the various environments students encounter outside school also intervene.

A Results Only Learning Environment eliminates the randomness that Guskey mentions and flattens the bell curve. As my classes continually demonstrate, no such curve exists in a ROLE. In fact, if I were to participate in the unsavory practice of placing my students on a geometrical shape, then they would land on something that looks like a staircase. In a given year, 5 percent of my students might receive a *D* or an *F* on their report cards, 20 percent might have a *C* or *C+*, 35 percent receive grades of *B* or *B+*, and the remaining 40 percent get *A*s. Each year, I try to flatten the staircase, just as I've flattened the bell. After all, if my students' achievement has to be measured by an insignificant letter, then I'm not sure why they can't all get an *A*.

When it comes to the high percentage of *A*s and *B*s my students typically average, the skeptic will say, "That's because you allow students to grade themselves. You don't assign homework, you have no worksheets, and test scores don't count against them." Of course, this is all true. Is this bad, though? Do I need a bell curve? Who benefits from it? The production, feedback, and change are what flatten the bell curve. The constant two-way feedback and performance reviews demonstrate students' learning. Skeptics want letters and GPAs. A results-only classroom may not provide these, but there are plenty of other far more valuable ways to evaluate learning that do not require grades. When a student enters my class as a reluctant reader and leaves as an avid reader, I know he or she has been successful. That student has developed a thirst for learning. Why should I crush this enthusiasm with punitive grades just to fill some spots on a bell curve?

If educators are truly willing to reform our broken system, then it's time to flatten the bell. A ROLE can change everything when it comes to grade distribution. Flattening the bell curve is one of the most thrilling experiences you'll ever have as an educator. Eliminate the punishment of points and percentages and let narrative feedback handle the rest. You'll be amazed by the results.

Evaluating While Evolving

The only man who behaves sensibly is my tailor; he takes my measurements anew every time he sees me, while all the rest go on with their old measurements and expect me to fit them.

—George Bernard Shaw

Narrative feedback, provided in a structured system such as SE2R, signals an evolution in the way teachers evaluate students. The days of placing a number or a letter at the top of a student's paper and blotting red ink all over the margins must come to an end if education is to move into the 21st century and beyond. However, since teachers have been conditioned since their preservice days to grade this way, they may need more than just a convenient system to help them move beyond 20th century assessment.

There are many formal and informal ways both to provide narrative feedback to students and to get feedback in return. Student feedback drives instruction and project creation, as it helps teachers distinguish gaps in learning. All feedback, no matter how it's delivered or received, helps with the evaluation of learning, but much of the feedback I provide and that my students give back to me takes place via some sort of interactive technology. We live in a digital age, and students want to be on computers. Meeting them on their playing field makes the process of evaluation and feedback easy.

This chapter outlines a collection of feedback methods I like to call my feedback toolkit (see Figure 6.1). You may already use some of these techniques, but most teachers do not consider all of them part of evaluation. Remember, the most basic conversation with a student after simple observation of an activity can supply valuable feedback that will help you evaluate mastery of learning outcomes and open the student's eyes to his or her own accomplishments. Observation and two-way narrative feedback are the ultimate methods of assessment. Noted education researcher Stephen Krashen clarifies this point when he says, "The repeated judgments of professionals who are with children every day is more valid than a test created by distant strangers. Moreover, teacher evaluations are 'multiple measures,' are closely aligned with the curriculum, cover a variety of subjects, and are 'value-added,' that is, they take improvement into consideration" (2011b, p.17). When reviewing the contents of the feedback toolkit, consider how easy it is to supply meaningful evaluation, while allowing students to make changes, so you can see how much value has been added or if mastery has been achieved.

Student Websites

As indicated earlier, I use a classroom website that hosts presentation materials, videos, my instructional blog, our interactive syllabus, message board, student blog, and, most important, private student websites. For a quick look at my classroom website, use your smartphone to scan the QR code provided in Figure 6.2. Student sites, contained in an alphabetical content management system on the classroom website, are an integral piece of our Results Only Learning Environment; they house projects and are one of our largest platforms for evaluation. The feedback examples I shared in Chapter 2 were placed on private

6.1 | Feedback Toolkit

Tool	Description
Student Websites	A wiki or other content management system (CMS) is best for creating private student websites. Students can place any activity or project on the pages they create, and the teacher can supply feedback that no one else can see.
Online Message Board	The classroom message board can be contained on your classroom website, or it can be a standalone site (e.g., ProBoards.com). The message board provides a powerful outlet for students to comment on classroom and one another's topics and to communicate privately with the teacher. (This is especially helpful for shy students who are afraid to raise their hands in class.)
Classroom Blog	Hosted by an education site (e.g., KidBlog), this is another CMS that allows students to share content. Teachers can supply public or private feedback and control what content is seen by a student's peers. Best of all, each blogger's peers can provide comments, which is another powerful form of feedback.
Online Grade Book	This is typically used for points and letter grades, but most have a comments section. Since students and parents are conditioned by other teachers to find grades on the online grade book, they can also locate narrative feedback there.
Google Drive	Formerly Google Docs, Google Drive is a collaborative online document sharing system that allows students to share any document with a teacher or peer. The powerful comment stream makes two-way narrative feedback easy.
Sidebar	Although it looks like a simple conversation, the sidebar is one of the sharpest tools in the feedback toolkit. This is a one-to-one chat, out of earshot of peers, that makes a connection to learning.
Other web-based tools	Most websites and applications have some way to provide feedback. Students can complete various tasks and receive feedback from peers or teachers. Some examples are Animoto, Diigo, Edmodo, Facebook, Glogster, Goodreads, Twitter, Voki, and Wikispaces.

student websites. My students love their websites because they enjoy the freedom to develop the sites any way they wish, while maintaining other activities and year-long projects in a safe place.

6.2 | QR Code for Classroom Website Example

The websites create a paperless project environment that allows students to work at their own pace and collect ongoing feedback from me. They can set up e-mail alerts, so they'll know when I've left something for them. As the school year progresses, though, they become accustomed to seeking out my comments on their websites without being prompted. Best of all, the websites encourage students to make immediate changes to their work (which is impossible with traditional paper-based activities). Sometimes, I link feedback to a minilesson or video from class so students can review that material before returning to their own websites to make changes that indicate they've mastered the objectives. The student websites make a new version of all saved pages, automatically creating a web-based portfolio that can be reflected on later in the school year.

Student websites are perfect examples of learning in a results-only classroom. The main class site provides a library of resources, which students can use as they see fit, and the private pages give students a platform to demonstrate learning in many ways. They also create unique learning environments that can be filled with personal pictures and designed with students' own text colors, font styles, and attachments.

Although student pages are private, creating a one-to-one student-teacher setting, work can be shared in computer labs or via an interactive whiteboard (or a traditional whiteboard with a projector), giving students a sense of community, even in this semiprivate online world.

Online Message Board

To make communication easy, our online message board is embedded directly into our classroom website. Students quickly learn a simple web address—www.barnesclass.com—and they know they can communicate with me there on our message board. The message board plays two key roles. One board is a library of class activities. A truly remarkable web-based tool, the classroom message board can be manipulated in a variety of ways that help with organization. I like to create separate topics for each class, even if the activity is the same. For example, I might use the classroom board to get feedback on books that students are currently reading. I teach five sections of language arts per day, so I'll create five topics on the classroom board, identified by class period. The board would then contain topics such as "Period 1 current book titles" or "Period 7 goals." When students click the appropriate link, they get more information—for example, "Post the book you are currently reading, its genre and author, and anything else you wish to add." Then I create others for each of my remaining four classes. I teach my students early in the year to be sure to post in the proper topic, so I can easily locate all students and evaluate their work. The classroom board is also useful as a discussion board where students can converse about any topic related to our class. This works well for engaging students who are typically reluctant to participate. All my students love the classroom message board, and it's a marvelous evaluation tool for me since I get specific feedback from my students on a variety of topics.

The second board is used for one-to-one, private communication between individual students and me. The "Write to Mr. Barnes" board has a built-in security feature that separates students by username. They can then write to me privately about a class issue, with a question about a project, to ask for feedback on something, or to reflect on their own progress. No other student will see what is written to me on this private board. I am always finding creative ways to use the private message board. Although I like to meet with students at the end of each grading period to discuss a final report card grade (something I cover further in Chapter 7), I may ask them to replace the face-to-face chat later in the year with a self-evaluation, which they place on our private message board. We meet in a computer lab or media center (they can also do this at home), and I preface the activity by telling them that I want them to reflect on the grading period and their production.

"What kind of work did you produce? How did you react to my feedback? Did you make the necessary changes to demonstrate mastery of our learning objectives?" Since we have no grades throughout the marking period, I explain that I have very little interest in the final letter grade, because I know what they've learned based on the results. However, I ask them to think about "the grade world" and how it functions.

"If you have missed any assignments (a rare occurrence) or neglected to use the feedback I've supplied on all projects and activities, then you have to assign a less-than-perfect grade, as this is the nature of the grade world." I refrain from putting too fine a point on this grade talk, because I really want students to make the final decision. From this point, they go to our web-based grade program, their private websites, the classroom blog, and our message board, where they review all the feedback they've received throughout the nine-week grading period. Invariably, this amounts to an immense amount of feedback. Finally, students go to our private message board and tell me what grade they believe they should have and why.

Classroom Blog

Like the private student websites and our message board, the blog is accessed through a link on our classroom website. Although the blog is a place for students to write about books and other class activities, it is also a wonderful venue for student feedback. Unlike private websites, most of the feedback I leave on blog posts is similar to what any objective viewer might leave. I comment on the content and sometimes leave a question. I often ask students to leave (positive) feedback for one another. I teach them early on how to leave effective constructive feedback that underscores only the positives of a peer's writing. Not only does this alleviate the risk of one student vilifying another for all to see, it also helps focus their attention on what's good about writing in general. Student blog comments are an integral part of the writing process; people always value the opinions of their peers. In addition, this evaluation process gets students thinking about their own writing. Here are two examples of student feedback on blog posts:

> **Yolanda:** John, there are many things I like about your reflection. One of my favorite things is how you took certain parts from the story and put it in your reflection. Another thing I liked is how you gave your opinion on what you think true friends are—"True friends should always be open with each other, ask for forgiveness, express feelings, listen to each other, put bad things behind them, and step into the other person's shoes in order to have a productive relationship."

> **Alisha:** Shelvin, I think this is a very good reflection letter. I like how you could connect and say what it reminded you of. I also like how you were saying what you could and could not relate to in the book. You also said how you can relate to Macy. So, I think this was a very good reflection letter.

The feedback that students give to their peers is another wonderful example of the effectiveness of a results-only class. My students willingly leave feedback for their peers. They don't do it for points or a grade. I tell them that their comments will help everyone improve, so they are eager to post them.

Online Grade Book

Obviously, this is a confusing heading, since we really have no grades in a Results Only Learning Environment. My school district, like many others, has an online grade book that is used to calculate quarterly grades and GPAs and to deposit homework assignments. If you have read more than a few sentences of this book, a computer program such as this one may seem like a useless tool for me. Surprisingly, our online grade book is probably where I leave the majority of my narrative feedback. Since students are taught from elementary school to access their grades online, they enter middle school with good knowledge of how the system functions. In no time, teachers condition students to log onto the program every time they boot up a computer. Since most teachers use a points-per-assignment system of grading, students quickly learn they can see their grades in real time, especially in classes with diligent educators who update the grade book daily.

So how does someone who never puts points or a letter on any activity and who never assigns homework use a program designed explicitly for these purposes? Instead of points, grades, or the word *missing* for incomplete assignments, I use the comments field, which is available for every student. It is adjacent to any activity the teacher creates (see Figure 6.3). Instead of seeing a grade, students and their parents click the Language Arts link on our online grade book and see a list of activities, diagnostics, and projects. Beside each activity, I provide the type of narrative feedback previously discussed. It took some time to get students and parents used to the idea that there was no grade, but by our open house (roughly one month into the school year), students understand and most parents are on board.

6.3 | Online Grade Book with Narrative Feedback

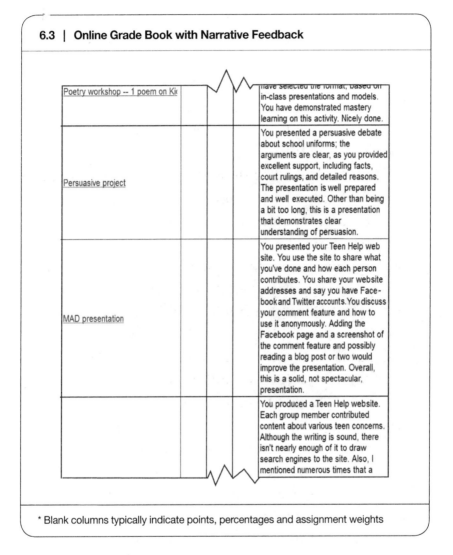

Poetry workshop -- 1 poem on Ki(				have selected the format, based on in-class presentations and models. You have demonstrated mastery learning on this activity. Nicely done.
Persuasive project				You presented a persuasive debate about school uniforms; the arguments are clear, as you provided excellent support, including facts, court rulings, and detailed reasons. The presentation is well prepared and well executed. Other than being a bit too long, this is a presentation that demonstrates clear understanding of persuasion.
MAD presentation				You presented your Teen Help web site. You use the site to share what you've done and how each person contributes. You share your website addresses and say you have Face-book and Twitter accounts. You discuss your comment feature and how to use it anonymously. Adding the Facebook page and a screenshot of the comment feature and possibly reading a blog post or two would improve the presentation. Overall, this is a solid, not spectacular, presentation.
				You produced a Teen Help website. Each group member contributed content about various teen concerns. Although the writing is sound, there isn't nearly enough of it to draw search engines to the site. Also, I mentioned numerous times that a

* Blank columns typically indicate points, percentages and assignment weights

Teachers are conditioned to believe that everything students produce has to be assessed. A simple one-minute math problem therefore gets a check or a meaningless score of 4/5. The teacher may even stroll around the room as students work on the activity and place these marks on papers over the students' shoulders. I used to do this. It was a pointless, utilitarian method then, and it remains so today. If your school has an online grade book, you can replace the checks and numbers with a much more meaningful comment. Carry a clipboard around the room with you and, instead of marking students' papers (a potentially embarrassing procedure for them), make a simple designation on your class roster or seating chart, indicating how the student performed on the activity.

I use my own, basic shorthand system that you can easily use as a template (see Figure 6.4). When translating the designations into our online grade book, I type the feedback for one student, copy and paste it into the comment field for all students who received that same designation. Therefore, if I'm evaluating our focused free write—a timed writing activity that gives students a chance to reflect or predict—then I'm really looking to see that the basic guidelines of this routine activity are followed. Leaving feedback on an activity such as this isn't always necessary, but since students like to see feedback in their online grade book, I occasionally leave it. As I navigate the pods of desks unobtrusively (my presence should be unnoticed by students, if possible), I make brief notes next to names on my seating chart. Most students get a designation of ML, which means "mastery learning demonstrated." Some may get a mark of T?2, which translates to "full time not used; wrote for two of three minutes." Others get ND, or "needs detail."

When you have time in your day, expand your shorthand system into narrative feedback and place it in your online grade book. This can be as easy and repetitive as your point system. If your simple in-class activity is worth five points, then most students might get 5/5. Instead of registering a bunch of 5s with a smattering of 3s and 4s, type one comment that indicates exactly what was done right on the activity. For example, a math teacher might say, "You correctly found the area by multiplying length times width. Congratulations on mastering this problem." That teacher could then simply copy this feedback and paste it into the comment section of any student who mastered the activity. It's far more rewarding for students to see exactly what they've accomplished, and parents will be much happier when they see a narrative

6.4 | Shorthand System for Quick Narrative Feedback

ACTIVITY: FOCUSED FREE WRITE

Designation	Narrative Feedback for Online Grade Book
ML (Mastery learning demonstrated)	You completed a three-minute focused free write on rhythm and rhyme in poetry. You then shared your thoughts with peers in your small group. You have demonstrated mastery understanding of the focused free write activity.
T?2 (Full time not used; wrote for two of three minutes)	You wrote for roughly two of the three minutes that were allotted for this activity. It's important that you write for the full time, as this is an integral part of the focused free write guidelines. Remember, you can always repeat your last thought until a new one comes to mind. Please do this on our next free write.
ND (Needs detail)	Although you wrote for the entire three minutes, you only restated the definition of rhythm and rhyme that was shared in class. It's okay to repeat thoughts when you are stuck, but you didn't do this; rather, you reworded the same sentence numerous times, making it difficult for me to see that you comprehend this concept. Please write a paragraph, summarizing rhythm and rhyme, based on what we learned in class, and place it on your website. Let me know when it's finished.

explanation of success rather than a meaningless 5/5. For students who get the activity wrong, the comment can indicate the problem. Redirect students to a prior lesson or textbook page, or invite them for extra help. When they demonstrate mastery, return to this activity in your online grade book and change the comment. When you and your students revisit the grade book around final grade time, this feedback will play an instrumental role in determining the report card grade, if one is necessary.

Google Drive

Many of my students use Google Drive (formerly Google Docs) for year-long projects. Although our classroom website allows for two-way narrative feedback and private comments from teacher to student, Google Drive provides a powerful platform for commenting within a document at the precise place where feedback is most relevant (see Figure 6.5). This application also contains a highlighting tool that helps the project designer see exactly where problems exist, based on what a peer editor or teacher has done. In addition, there is a comment stream at the top of each document that makes it easy for students to access all feedback. The student can then respond, which is especially effective for alerting the teacher or collaborator to any changes that have been made.

What makes Google Drive particularly effective, beyond these utilities, is its inherent ability to spark intrinsic motivation, based on the immediacy of the feedback. When students know they will get a quick response from a teacher on their hard work, their motivation to continue the project grows. Here is one example of ongoing feedback I left on Google Drive for a student who was writing a novel for our year-long Make a Difference project:

> You have so much to be proud of here. This story is so filled with life and passion. It's clear that you believe in it and want it to be something special. I think you are creating truly publishable work here. I haven't read it all yet, but from what I have read, I see that it's growing and improving. Your writing is getting better with each page. Your mechanics are vastly improved from the beginning of the school year. I made a comment in the section called "LIFE." Keep an eye out for this type of feedback, as it will help you sharpen your skills. Meanwhile, keep your eye on the prize—a published work.

The student in question was my student in both 7th and 8th grades. If she had told me she wanted to write a novel at the beginning of her 7th

6.5 | Student Document on Google Drive with Embedded Teacher Comments

When I was young, I always wanted to be my mother. There were times when I wanted to be a lot of people. I was never popular in school. I never had many friends and everyone thought I was a freak in clothes, which I was, in every ones opinion except my mom's. She always loved me unconditionally. So for almost every moment I wanted to be her. I wanted to know how it felt to love myself, to care

grade year, I would have envisioned a few pages of conflicting ideas that would have taken the entire year to edit just to make the work readable. Her writing skills were, at best, poor. The fact that she didn't like to read made helping her improve her skills quite challenging. Year-long projects and ongoing feedback, though, aided this student in her remarkable progress over a two-year period. By the end of her 7th grade year, she had become an avid reader, and her writing was becoming more detailed and creative. Three-quarters of the way through her 8th grade year, though, she was a different student entirely. Books became an escape where she not only found engaging characters and ideas but also developed a passion for storytelling.

One month after committing to writing a novel of her own, this previously reluctant reader and writer had penned more than 15,000 well-crafted words of an intriguing novel. She looked forward to the narrative feedback in her Google Drive comment stream, made changes accordingly, and worked feverishly to complete the project by the end of the school year. Heading into high school, she was a young novelist, publishing her work on the Internet for the world to see. Not once in two years did I place a number or letter grade on her work.

Sidebar

The sidebar is not a revolutionary creation; it's just a simple name I use for a practice many good teachers have been using for decades. A sidebar is a one-to-one teacher-student chat that may or may not be related to a class activity. It is, however, critical to the success of a ROLE and a powerful feedback tool. The workshop setting that a results-only classroom embraces lends itself to plenty of interaction between the teacher and students. As noted earlier, while my students work, I'm constantly on the move, joining small groups and individuals. This is a perfect time for the sidebar. Not only do these individual chats provide two-way feedback, they are also excellent rapport builders.

Many of my students come from single-parent homes, and they are responsible for household chores and, in many cases, babysitting a younger sibling. Remaining after school for help is often not possible. One-to-one conversations, though, are still necessary. Rather than invite a student to stay after school to discuss a project or anything else, I handle these discussions with sidebars, which can take place in the classroom, in a cafeteria, at a student's locker, or strolling down the hallway. Sometimes, I even pull a student from another class for a two-minute sidebar. Witness the value of the sidebar and two-way feedback in the following examples.

Shonda's Story

At the beginning of our Reading All Year unit, I deal with numerous reluctant readers. Shonda was one. We were reading silently one day, and Shonda had her head down and was not reading. She was sitting in the back of the room, isolated from her group. I knelt beside her desk and whispered, "What's wrong? Do you feel okay?"

"I'm okay," Shonda responded. "I just don't like reading."

When promoting individual reading to students who have read very little in their lives, the beginning of a year-long reading project is a delicate matter. "You know what?" I began, "When I was your age, I didn't like to read either." I didn't become an avid reader until I got to college. Shonda sat up, curious about a language arts teacher who wasn't born with a book in his hands. "It's true," I continued. "I was too busy playing with friends and watching TV to be bothered with books. Plus, no one explained the amazing world that books would reveal to me."

This sidebar continued quietly, and while others read or whispered about their books, I convinced Shonda to browse our classroom library for something that interested her. I have over 1,000 young adult novels and nonfiction books in my classroom, and this easy access is critical to the success of students such as Shonda who often are not exposed to books outside of school. "I have concluded that reading for pleasure, self-selected reading, is the major cause of literacy development. Making sure that all children have access to books makes literacy development possible. Without it, literacy development is impossible" (Krashen, 2011a).

Shonda and I diligently surveyed the mountains of titles on my shelves. Eventually, she settled on a short novel, *Monkey Island*, and labored to read it over the next three weeks. When Shonda finished that book, she was eager to tell me she had done so. She wrote the title in our Celebrating Reading journal, and I later added it to our online slide show, which is played on a large TV outside our media center for the entire school to view. Shonda became one of my class librarians, and her interest in reading exploded. Nearly four months after our brief sidebar, she lingered after class one day, waiting for everyone else to leave. She came to me with a broad smile and eagerly announced that she had just finished reading her 17th book. I asked her how many books she had read in a single year prior to that one. "Maybe three," she said.

I certainly can't take credit for Shonda's discovery of the avid reader buried inside her, but a simple sidebar in which I shared a revealing personal story may have been the catalyst that nudged her toward the wonderful world of reading. That year, Shonda was a 7th grader. The following year, even though I had been moved to the 8th grade, she was no longer my student. I bumped into her occasionally, though, and sometimes she even stopped by my room after school, just to say hello and, of course, borrow books.

Jennifer's Story

Jennifer spent much of the first grading period missing class and producing very little. When she wasn't absent, she offered a few insightful observations during small-group or whole-class discussions, and she asked some higher-level thinking questions, leading me to believe that she was underachieving. Her writing was reckless for an honors-level student, lacking focus and revision. I wasn't sure what was wrong with Jennifer, and colleagues and counselors had nothing else to offer about her academically or personally. Her absences were excused, as she had been sick intermittently. I spoke with a parent at our open house, and there were no concerns at home. I was informed that Jennifer had always been a good student prior to middle school.

One class period, as our cooperative teams aggressively debated issues related to a short story we were reading, I casually beckoned Jennifer to my desk, away from earshot of her peers. (I do this so often that students pay little mind to one-to-one chats during class.) "You have me very confused," I told Jennifer. "All indications are that you should be producing excellent work, yet your projects are hardly touched, and you have not completed several in-class activities that we did while you were absent." This was our first sidebar, and Jennifer didn't know how to respond; she stood quietly staring at the floor. "If I asked you to grade yourself right now," I probed, "what do you think you would say?" Reluctantly, she said the grade would be an *F*. I explained that I was not interested in letter grades and that we only had to have a final grade on a report card. "However, I do care that you produce. You know that we work in a Results Only Learning Environment, which means you need to produce, get feedback from me, and make changes when needed. If you do nothing, I can't leave feedback, and neither of us can see that you've learned anything."

Jennifer said she hadn't thought of it this way, but she promised to improve her projects and complete any missing activities. A few weeks later, it was time for quarterly self-evaluation. In the meantime, Jennifer had completed a major project and several missing activities. She was proud of her progress. I told her I was happy to see her production improve, but I still had to evaluate her work and leave feedback. Before she could complete her final assessment, she would have to see my feedback and make necessary changes. A few days later, we spoke again. Jennifer had made some changes to individual activities but had done little to her major project. "So where are we?" I inquired. Jennifer considered her grade and decided on a *C*. "I turned in a lot of stuff late," she said, "and I didn't have time to make all of the changes you wanted, but I still plan to do it later."

This one brief sidebar encouraged Jennifer to produce and give herself an average final grade. Best of all, she made changes to her project a few weeks later, even though the marking period had ended. The grade was meaningless to her. She wanted to prove to me and, more important, to herself that she had learned. This was a ROLE student if there ever was one.

Aleya's Story

Aleya was a classic at-risk student. She had failing grades in almost all subjects over several marking periods. She assigned herself an *F* in the first two marking periods for my class. When evaluating progress at the beginning of the second semester, I realized Aleya was slipping through the cracks. Although almost every student of mine was now thriving in our results-only classroom and workshop setting, Aleya still was not producing. A quiet child, happy to blend into the background, she was content with a report card littered with *F*s—yet another solid example of a failing education system. At the onset of the third quarter, I decided it was time to press Aleya. One day, I kept her after the ending bell, as I had no students during the class period after hers. Aleya was immediately frustrated; she didn't do well with confrontation. Slouching in her chair and avoiding eye contact, it was clear she wanted no part of this conversation.

"Aleya, I want to help you, but you are making it difficult for me," I began. "All I want is some production, but you give none. It isn't like there are parts of projects missing; you have ignored them completely." She wasn't even working during class time, which is unheard of in our workshop setting. "I need your help," I implored. "How are we going to turn this thing around?" Aleya looked surprised. I got the feeling that no one had ever asked for her opinion on how to change her direction. More likely, she had only been told what to do and threatened with summer school or retention. Finally, after lengthy contemplation, Aleya whispered shyly that she wanted to complete activities, but she was sometimes confused with instructions and didn't know how to get started on projects. Her feedback during this five-minute sidebar helped me better understand how to help her. Aleya wanted to succeed, but she didn't quite know how to begin. For the remainder of that school year, Aleya was a different student. I checked in on her more regularly, often breaking large tasks into smaller ones. Sometimes I'd just drop by, sit next to her, and ask what she was reading and how she liked it. She started completing all activities and projects and was reading more than ever.

For the last two grading periods, Aleya received 10 grades in five classes. In four traditional points-and-letters classes, she got seven *F*s and a *D*. After giving herself *F*s in the first two marking periods in language arts, she improved to *C*s in the second semester. If I had graded her in the final marking period, she would have received a *B*.

7

Reviewing Performance

True genius resides in the capacity for evaluation of uncertain, hazardous, and conflicting information.

—*Winston Churchill*

The problem with the office performance reviews in the private sector, according to Daniel Pink (2009), is that they often come six months after the work is complete, cheating the employee from detailed, constructive, and immediate feedback. This sort of after-the-fact performance review is similar to the end-of-the-marking-period letter grade that we foist off on students, rarely considering its long-term ramifications. Students work for nine weeks, or maybe twice that, depending on whether the school year is divided into quarters or semesters. Granted, students may receive grades on individual activities or projects that ultimately compose their final grades, but the fact of the matter is that, at the end of a lengthy period of production, our "employees" still get a performance review that is often uncomfortable and is, at best, an insufficient summary of what they actually did.

As I have reiterated throughout previous chapters, letter grades demonstrate nearly nothing about real learning and academic achievement. In order to evaluate learning and provide legitimate feedback to students and parents, a lengthier, more detailed review of our students' performance is necessary. A Results Only Learning Environment gives students constant feedback throughout the year, and it culminates in the final performance review. Like the letter grade, an oral or written performance review is a summation of what each student has accomplished. Unlike the letter grade, performance reviews are not punitive, and they offer detailed information about what each student accomplished during a grading period. What follows are several kinds of performance reviews with real examples from my classes.

Quarterly Self-Evaluation

Some teachers have been using student self-evaluations for years. For them, this process is a critical part of deciding final report card grades. Joe Bower, a well-known education writer, teaches a variety of subjects and grade levels in Alberta, Canada, and he threw out number and letter grades years ago. Unless assigning a grade at the end of a marking period, which is mandated by his school district (just as it is by most districts in the United States), Bower uses various kinds of feedback. "I am the kind of teacher who strongly believes in creating an environment where students can experience success and failure not as reward and punishment, but as information. . . . We don't spend one minute more than we need to discussing the grades—in turn, this de-emphasis on grading allows my students to be attracted to learning for its own sake" (Bower, 2011, para. 6, 7).

Other teachers, though new to this philosophy, are quickly learning how rewarding self-evaluation can be for both teacher and student. Mark McGunagle, who teaches English at Westwood High School in Massachusetts, discovered results-only learning in 2011, and he began developing his own ROLE shortly thereafter. "Because this is the first real attempt at a ROLE, and students haven't participated in real self-evaluation before, we had to create a kind of hybrid to fit our situation." McGunagle wanted to change how the public speaking class at his school was taught, so he decided to include student self-evaluation as the primary method of assessment. Since the experience was new to him and his students, McGunagle developed a rubric to ease the transition from grading to self-evaluation. However, like Bower, McGunagle wanted to decrease the emphasis on grading. "In the future, our goal is to eliminate the rubric of preparedness, participation, classroom presence, and punctuality; instead, we'll define (as a class) the criteria for each of these course components. Then, at the end of each term, we'll have a similar evaluation handout, but without the rubric. Instead, students will think of the criteria and goals for each component, then write a narrative describing their performance." As students' self-evaluation of their own performance evolves over the course of a school year, the creation of evaluative tools, such as McGunagle's rubric, become unnecessary.

During the first quarter of the year, I ask all students to complete a self-evaluation. This is not always a guided activity, although it can be. I've had groups of students that were so good at self-evaluation that they never needed any help; they simply reviewed their work and my feedback, and deciding on a grade was not a problem. Some students, however, need assistance. "I don't know how to do this," they'll say. A simple self-evaluation form helps narrow their focus and gets them on track. Although I hate putting points on anything, I have used a scaled rating on self-evaluation forms to guide students (see Figure 7.1). Of course, we always decide together what grade is fair.

Since going to results-only learning, I'm no longer a fan of weighting activities. Weighting ultimately involves judging how much work students invest, and effort is something that is far too abstract to judge. However, our year-long projects are certainly more valuable than other things we do. This isn't because of the amount of work the projects require as much as it's about the many learning outcomes that the

7.1 | Final Grading Period Self-Evaluation

Student:_____ Date:_____

Class period: _____ Final grade: _____

Instructions: Begin by reviewing all activities and feedback. Did you miss any activities, diagnostics, or parts of any project? If you did, this impacts your report card grade.

After reviewing all activities and feedback, give yourself a 0–5 rating, based on how well you've done in each area. Then use the suggested grade section to determine your final grade, and place that grade on the line above. Bring this sheet to our evaluation conference.

Category

Year-long projects:	0	1	2	3	4	5
In-class activities:	0	1	2	3	4	5
Collaboration:	0	1	2	3	4	5
Team projects:	0	1	2	3	4	5
Diagnostics:	0	1	2	3	4	5
Meeting goals:	0	1	2	3	4	5

What report card grade should I have? Consider the following:

- All 4s and 5s merit a high report card grade.
- Remember, year-long projects are more important than other categories. Excellent work on these could outweigh a couple 3s in other categories.
- Similarly, if you have 5s in four categories, but you have a 3 in year-long projects, this would lower your final grade at least one letter.
- A combination of 3s and 4s would put your grade at a C or lower.

project envelops. A diary project, for example, involves a significant amount of research on top of multiple reading and writing objectives. A one-day newspaper activity might capture only three or four objectives. Hence, my self-evaluation sheet emphasizes this point and encourages students to consider their projects more heavily than in-class activities that are unrelated to the projects. I also add collaboration to my self-evaluation sheet. This is obviously far too subjective to grade, but I want my students to consider how good they are at it, since collaboration is such a huge part of our classroom environment. Having students rate themselves on collaboration or discuss it in our one-to-one conference heightens their awareness of how adept they are at working with others. My ultimate goal is for my students to be able to evaluate themselves without the use of a structured form, but it doesn't always work out this way; some students just feel more comfortable with the guidance of an evaluation tool.

The evaluation form is especially useful for elementary school teachers. Since most K–3 teachers have only one group of students, it should be easy to sit down with students individually and help them with a checklist, while discussing the value of what has been learned and what areas need more attention during the next grading period. Even five-year-olds can handle this sort of self-evaluation, and the process reinforces the autonomy you are teaching, compelling students to take charge of their own learning. If a positive spin can be placed on obsession, then being obsessed with one's own learning is certainly a positive thing that should begin at a very early age.

Individual Meetings

During self-evaluation, my students are instructed to use our online grade book along with our message board, our blog, and their private websites to review what they've accomplished. I then meet with students individually to discuss their conclusions and complete our performance review. Notice, I said *our* review. At the end of each marking period, I believe it's of paramount importance that students realize I play a role in their learning, but that it is ultimately *their* learning. Hence, the final grade that goes on a report card will be one they select. If you are skeptical about students being able to handle this, recall the example of Sasha from the Introduction. After her self-evaluation and our combined

review of her performance, Sasha said that her final grade had to be an
F. She was not my only student who decided on low grades throughout
the year. In fact, in any given grading period, many students assign
themselves lower grades than they received the prior marking period.
These are teenagers who have been given complete control over their
report card grades, yet many literally give themselves lower grades
than their peers receive and, in some cases, poor grades that are not
popular with parents. There is integrity to this process, which, I believe,
is strengthened throughout the year as students constantly consider
their own learning.

There may be times that you and a student initially disagree on the
grade. The letter itself doesn't matter much to me, as I'm a firm believer
that schools should discard the letter grade system completely. I do,
however, think that students should be honest in evaluating their own
performance, which is extremely difficult for some of them (indeed, many
adults are not good at it). After all, from roughly 2nd grade, students have
been conditioned to think that grades are important, and even those who
have historically received low grades want high ones. I give students the
opportunity to give themselves the grades they want, so there are occasions when a student will desire a grade that is higher than he or she
deserves, based on how a traditional grading system functions.

Let's suppose a student says, "I think I deserve a *B+*," when his
or her performance indicates something lower. I'll furrow an eyebrow
and respond, "Hmm." A considerable pause sends the student back to
reflection. "Let's think about this some more," I'll add. We then revisit
the online grade book. Perhaps my feedback on an ongoing project
asked the student to return to one specific activity and make a change
after reviewing an online presentation. Alternatively, perhaps I asked
the student to see me individually for some extra help on a particular
activity. "Remember, when I asked you to come to me for extra help?"
I'll inquire. "You never came, so there was no change to the project. I

can't tell that you mastered this concept." At this point—99 percent of the time—the student says, "Oh, you're right. I guess I don't deserve a *B*+." Better still, students will often say, "Can I still change the project?" Even if they do this only because they want a better report card grade, it still provides an opportunity to learn.

Sometimes students still won't agree with your suggestions, either because they haven't learned the results-only system yet or because they are receiving pressure from home to get "good grades." They want the *A*, even when you explain that they don't deserve it. If you have started the year by allowing your students to decide their final report card grade, then it's critical you honor this. Remember, students won't believe in a ROLE if you are not true to your word all the time. When teaching in a high school, where students rely on their GPA to get into college, this can become a bit tricky. If you are concerned that students are under too much pressure to handle this responsibility, then you can take their feedback and use it as part of your own performance review before *you* decide on the final grade. At lower levels, though, it's much easier to allow students to grade themselves, which is what I do.

For example, a student once told me at the end of a grading period that she wanted an *A*. Her poor project work would have placed her in the *C*+ or *B*– range in the points-and-percentages world. I explained this to her, using numbers to demonstrate how the percentage of her completed activities would likely fall somewhere around 80 percent if we were using a points system. "Seeing this, do you still want the *A*?" I asked. She did. This was a first, and I was perplexed and even a bit frustrated. I asked if all she cared about was a letter on a report card. "Does what you've produced really mean that little to you?" She paused and contemplated my words. I felt certain she'd reconsider. "So?" I coaxed. She looked at me and said, "I want the *A*." I put the grade in our online system and told her she could return to her seat. "You're going to give me the *A*?" she asked in a surprised voice. I nodded. "I told you it means nothing to me," I said. "It's obviously important to you, though." She returned to her seat without saying anything else. For the remainder of the school year, this student did marvelous work and deserved high grades every marking period. Although I never asked her about it, I truly believe she increased her effort because she came to understand what results-only learning is really about. If I had gone back on my word and given her a lower grade that quarter, then she would never have trusted me and, I believe to this day, her drive toward mastery learning would have been stifled indefinitely.

Online Evaluation

After meeting individually for performance review in the first two quarters the first year I taught in a ROLE, I decided to have my students complete a self-evaluation for the third grading period using the private message board system. I wanted to see if their evaluations and grades would be dramatically impacted without a face-to-face discussion. Following are a few examples of self-evaluations and performance summaries, including direct quotes from students.

Malcolm: An *A* student throughout the year in most subjects, Malcolm had excelled in all areas of language arts, and we had happily agreed that he deserved a final grade of *A* on his report card in both of the first two quarters. During the third marking period, we had tackled our challenging research project. Students were allowed to choose partners to complete the research and final paper. Malcolm and his team struggled from the beginning. I had several sidebars with them, explaining that I felt they were not producing because they were spending too much valuable research time socializing. This, of course, was out of character for Malcolm. The team rebounded nicely and completed a solid, if unspectacular, research project. Malcolm knew this had hurt his overall performance in the third quarter. It is important to note that Malcolm was in my so-called regular Language Arts class, but we had agreed after the first semester that he would be placed in the advanced track during 8th grade.

On the day of the self-evaluation and performance write-ups, here is what Malcolm sent me on our private message board: "I don't think I did as good as I did the last two quarters. This quarter I slacked a little on my work as well. I also wasn't that wise on my partner choosing this quarter. I will do better next quarter to show you I am an advanced language arts student. I'm sorry Mr. Barnes; I let you and myself down. I agreed on giving myself a *B+*."

I responded to his message, telling him that I was proud of his maturity and that I was not disappointed in him. Malcolm was one of 33 students (31 percent of my combined class rosters) to assign a lower grade than what he had the previous quarter. Can you imagine students grading their performance lower than they got during the prior marking period, when given the chance? In a ROLE, it's not uncommon.

Lexy: Although I no longer need letter grades to demonstrate learning from one grading period to the next, Lexy has always been one of my favorite grade stories. When my colleagues first learned that I had abandoned traditional grading, most were skeptical. They assumed that if I allowed students to grade themselves, they would immediately award themselves *A*s and *B*s. Teachers are always shocked when I tell them that most students are more critical than their teachers, when they are coached on intrinsic motivation and given a fair chance to demonstrate their learning. A marvelous example of this almost uncanny integrity, Lexy was the kind of student teachers boast about. "Isn't she great?" numerous teachers would rhetorically ask when her name came up in various conversations about students we had in common. Lexy turned in all activities and typically worked very hard on projects. She even e-mailed me late in the school year to ask about a particular book in which she was interested, telling me that because of our Reading All Year project, she was reading more books than she ever had. After the first two grading periods, Lexy and I eagerly agreed that she deserved an *A* on her report card.

Like Malcolm, Lexy stumbled on the research project. Unlike Malcolm, though, she didn't recover. In spite of numerous sidebars with Lexy and her partner, a student who had not excelled throughout the year and had struggled with large projects, the research never took off. They got a very late start with their sources, notes, and outline. When it was time to post the paper to our online program, theirs never materialized. When I asked about it, Lexy told me she had written part of it without her partner's help and was struggling to post it to our research website. I, of course, told her I would help if needed. She declined, saying she would figure it out. I gave her the benefit of the doubt, based on her exemplary first-semester work, but the paper never appeared.

When it came time for self-evaluation, here is what Lexy wrote to me on our private message board: "Mr. Barnes, I think my grade should be nothing higher than a *D*. I don't think I did as well as I could have this quarter, because I didn't do very well on my research project. I did type a paper, but it didn't save. I know that we aren't going to work on it anymore, but I will get it done just to show you that I know how to collect research."

This was an *A* student who graded herself down to a *D*. It's also one more perfect example of how self-evaluations and performance reviews can easily and more effectively replace points and letters on assignments and projects. If I had graded my students using traditional points and percentages that school year, then my grade for Lexy might have been a *C*. Obviously, she would have received a failing grade on research, but she did enough of the remaining activities and projects to merit an average grade. Lexy's case makes it easy to see why narrative feedback and performance reviews constitute a much more effective method of evaluating students.

Final Teacher Performance Review

In my utopian vision of U.S. schools, *grading period* would be an archaic phrase that has been replaced with *quarterly performance review*. Long-time traditional teachers, tired of what they do and ready for retirement, would likely struggle in this place because it would remove all of the previously mentioned crutches that make the job of educating easy—especially grades created by numbers and percentages. Instead, teachers in my perfect schools would write lengthy, detailed narratives at the end of each evaluation cycle—maybe two or three times a year. These narratives would basically be expanded versions of the feedback students receive throughout each quarter or semester. Sadly, our current education system, which is built on outdated teaching methods and standardized tests, does not provide the time that this kind of evaluation requires. If you adopt a results-only system, however, performance reviews will play a large role in your yearly teaching agenda.

When I transitioned my class to a ROLE, I knew my students would receive a final grade and GPA, but I realized that without some sort of narrative summation of all the feedback they receive during the year, my part in their learning would be incomplete. My final performance review is a summary of what individual students have accomplished and how they have progressed in key language arts areas such as reading, writing, public speaking, group interaction, and year-long projects. The reports are written primarily to parents, but the personal pronoun *you* is used often, in order to maintain student interest. Writing these performance reviews is a time-consuming, but invaluable, procedure. In the following section, I'll share a few examples of actual reports I've written for past students. Later in this chapter, I'll talk about ways to get this monumental task finished and discuss what student self-reviews look like.

The first example was for a student who was in one of my regular Language Arts classes. She read and wrote below grade level and would be considered at-risk in most academic areas. As I indicated in my final report, I believe she would have failed in a traditional classroom and been placed in summer school—a horrible place that rarely teaches kids anything other than to hate school more than they probably already do. This example is the only one that includes the first and last sections of the performance review, as these are template pieces that are primarily the same in all reports.

Michelle: Final Language Arts Performance Review

How It Works

Students have been evaluated daily throughout the school year in Language Arts in the areas of reading, writing, oral presentation, collaboration, and project-based learning. Rather than record number or letter grades on individual activities and projects, students receive detailed narrative feedback throughout the year. The following performance review is about the student named above.

Summary and Recommendations

Michelle had a very difficult year in Language Arts. Although she showed some enthusiasm for our first-semester diary project— writing a creative piece on post-slavery days—she didn't follow my specific instructions for improving the work. In fact, I encouraged Michelle to spend time with me after school working on her writing, but she never did. Michelle continued to struggle with the basic mechanics of writing all year, and this is an area of concern.

Michelle's reading diagnostic scores were low throughout the year, yet she was reluctant to retake assessments when asked. She produced enough individual assignments and project work to earn a grade of *C* in quarters one and two. After missing significant class time in quarter three, and failing to make up missed class activities, we agreed that she deserved a *D*. This shows maturity on her part, as it's always difficult for students to assign themselves low grades.

(Continued)

As the year progressed, Michelle never really worked on reading, and I was constantly encouraging her to create a reading plan as part of our year-long reading project, telling her how important reading is to all parts of her academics. Still, Michelle rarely read, and she didn't come close to meeting her reading goal for the semester. After completing the research portion of our major research project, Michelle and her group failed to submit a competent paper, making it difficult for me to evaluate her understanding of this challenging process. This was a negative trend. Michelle never recovered from her early struggles. In a traditional classroom with homework and a punitive grading system, I believe Michelle would have failed Language Arts and likely would have been sent to summer school. Our results-only learning environment, which focuses on projects, cooperative learning, and performance review, has helped Michelle. I hope she will use this experience to improve in all areas next year.

Finally

Please join me at the Mustang Book Club twice weekly beginning June 20, **11:30 a.m. to 12:00 p.m. on Mondays and Thursdays**. As stated above, you need to read more. Reading will help you improve all academic areas. Please stop by the library this summer, so we can discuss your reading plan and find books you will love. I hope to see you this summer at the library or around town.

Michelle's performance review is direct. I believe that it's important to be as positive as possible, but it's also critical to outline problem areas. In addition, since we still live in a world of grades, summer school, and retention, I always let students and parents know when a child might be punished by these traditional practices in the future.

The next performance review was written for an honors-level student who did an exemplary job throughout the year in all areas. In fact, she was arguably the best student I'd had in a few years. Reviewing the performance for a student such as this may seem easy, but it's important not to simply mail it in. You have to find strengths that the student hasn't already heard constantly from other teachers. It's even more important to add advice for improvement, which can be difficult for "star" students.

Sherese: Language Arts Performance Review

Summary and Recommendations

Sherese has a wide array of language arts skills, and she worked hard on honing them throughout the year. She is a very creative writer, as indicated by her diary project, in which she crafted characters from the Great Depression and developed them over a three-month period. Her writing improved throughout the work, as she focused on basic mechanics and improved vocabulary. Sherese did a wonderful job of taking my specific feedback and making solid corrections and additions to her project. Her reading comprehension, vocabulary, and writing assessments have been above average throughout the year, and she and her group produced a very nice research project, which is one of the most difficult units of the year. Sherese was an asset to both whole- and small-group discussions, offering insightful questions and answers. I could always count on her to "bail me out" if a discussion was failing.

Sherese was part of a group that spearheaded a club with the goal of eliminating bullying at school. This demonstrates not only a wonderful personal code of ethics but also a strong ability to translate this code to a community—a very mature skill. It's been a pleasure having Sherese in my Language Arts class.

(Continued)

When it comes to Language Arts, it's difficult to find many weaknesses in Sherese. I would recommend continued work on the mechanics of writing, as some basic mistakes do occasionally work their way into her prose. She should make sure to proofread before turning in any formal writing. Also, this may be nitpicking, but I'd like to see her read more. Although she met her reading goal for the second semester, her Lexile measure did decrease significantly, and many of her peers are reading much more. I'd like to see Sherese challenge herself with a bigger volume of books and some at higher Lexile measures. A librarian can help with this, as will our classroom website.

As you may have guessed while looking at the examples, writing year-end performance reviews is a monumental task. There are a few important things to consider, which will make the job a bit less daunting and make the reviews more useful to your students.

Let students read their reviews. For many students, the arrival of the report card can be a scary time—one that often sends kids scurrying to the mailbox, hoping to hide the document from parents who may be outraged by the results. Students should never be afraid of the final performance review. Rather than including it in a report card, I like to have it mailed home separately, making it special. I distribute the reports in class a few days before school ends. I encourage my students to read their performance reviews carefully and ask me any questions they might have. Then they put the reviews in envelopes, which they address and our school stamps and mails. This way, they know what's coming, and in almost every case, they are eager to have their parents read these detailed reports.

Work smart to save time. The first time a colleague learned of my performance reviews, she was stunned. "Wow, that's really admirable," she said. "I would never want to have to do it, though." This is not to say she is a bad teacher, because this particular colleague is a favorite among students and an excellent educator. Her issue, the one that most teachers would raise with performance reviews, is with that element we have the least of but covet the most—time. When it comes to teachers who have 80–130 students each year, performance reviews can be quite intimidating. I won't suggest that it can be done easily or quickly. I do, however, have a few tips for completing final performance reviews without losing your mind. In the end, though, you have to commit to the idea that this is one of the most important parts of a results-only classroom, and your students and parents will be forever thankful to you for taking so much valuable time to give them more than a single letter for all their hard work.

A good template is the biggest timesaver you can create. Consider all the parts of a performance review that will be repetitive for each student, and put them into the first one you write. Then save it forever. Your template may change over time, but a well-designed first review will make any tweaking you do later that much easier. Notice that my examples have similar parts. The heading, "How It Works," and "Finally" sections remain the same on most performance reviews, with the obvious exception of the student's name. Note how my "Finally" section is dedicated to promoting my summer book club. I want all students to attend, so the dates and times are critical. Most of my students develop excellent reading habits as part of our year-long reading project, so I say "you've developed strong reading habits that will help you improve in all academic areas." I have emphasized this throughout the year, so I think it's good for students and their parents to see this. If a student has not worked a reading plan or developed these habits, I can change that sentence with a word or two, maintaining most of the section.

Although I'm not a fan of lists, if you have very large classes and feel you can't create a unique middle section for each student, then you might consider adding a list of completed projects or assessments to your template. Then you can simply delete any that particular individuals don't do. This will definitely save you time, but I believe it detracts from the overall effectiveness of the report.

Borrow writing time. This may not be popular with principals, but it's nearly impossible to write performance reviews without using some class time. Teachers are told relentlessly that they should parade around the classroom, hovering over students like helium balloons with eyes and ears. You and I know there are often occasions we refer to as "down time." During down time, students are fully engaged in some activity that doesn't require teachers to circulate constantly. A movie, sustained silent reading, small-group activities, or mandatory standardized testing are just a few examples of times when students don't need teachers. I like to borrow these times to write performance reviews. Depending on the student, a single performance review can take anywhere from 8–15 minutes to write. In a 45-minute block with students heavily engaged in an activity that doesn't require much interaction with the teacher, you can certainly borrow 25–30 minutes for your reviews. Do this four or five times in one teaching day, and you might write 12–15 performance reviews within the structure of your work day. If you can borrow even three days in this fashion, then you could knock out close to half of your reviews. Obviously, you won't be able to do this very often, so you'll have to use some planning time to write.

Set goals for completion. If you allow them to become overwhelming, performance reviews can become an arduous task you will grow to detest, instead of being the rewarding process they should be. I avoid feeling overwhelmed by setting reasonable goals for completion. As the year draws to a close, I count the days to when I'll need to have all my performance reviews complete. (I usually do this in May.) If I have 20 school days left and 80 reviews to write, then I will set a daily goal. If I write four performance reviews during each of those 20 days, then I could easily meet that goal. Sometimes even this small number seems too difficult to complete. In that case, I include the remaining weekends and promise myself I'll write four or five total reports during the weekend—maybe three on Saturday and two on Sunday. Any dedicated teacher can work for an hour on the weekend. Sticking to this kind of program will easily get the task done, and it's the most rewarding project you'll complete during the entire school year.

Student Performance Review

Another way to end the school year with a performance review is to have students complete their own reviews. You can do this instead of a teacher-written performance review, which certainly saves time, or you can do both. A huge advantage to having students complete their own reviews is that it gives you a day to work while they write. A well-crafted student self-review should take an entire 45-minute class period, especially if it is done on the computer. I use my classroom website, providing students with a template they can copy onto their private websites (see Figure 7.2). Almost all students enjoy completing their own performance reviews. I would estimate that 80 percent of my students spend 30–50 minutes on their reviews, writing lengthy, detailed paragraphs about their accomplishments over the course of a nine-month school year.

Since the review in no way affects their final grade (I assure them that grades are finalized and turned in before they begin their reviews), students are even more honest and critical than they are during quarterly self-evaluations. The feedback I get from these year-end student self-reviews is invaluable. Much of what we do throughout the school year is covered in the reviews, and the detail that students supply about all facets of our class helps me tweak projects, activities, and even daily procedures. For example, when one of my 8th graders wrote that she didn't feel her Make a Difference project reached its potential because

7.2 | Performance Review

We have gone through an entire year of reading, projects, and in-class activities. It's time to review your performance. Beneath the bullet points in each category below, discuss your performance for the entire school year.

Reading All Year / 2,500 Book Challenge

Address these topics:

- Quarterly reading goals—Did you set them? Did you meet them? Did you maintain and follow a reading plan? How did you do it?

- Reflecting on reading—How often did you reflect? Did you connect personally? Was this process helpful?

- Sharing—Were you an active participant in book chats? Did you present any book talks? How did this part of RAY affect your reading?

- Improvement—How would you estimate your improvement in reading?

Year-Long Projects

Consider your collaborative efforts, your own enthusiasm, your time management, and specific things you learned.

- Max Teaching/Avid work

- Diigo

- Make a Difference (MAD)

- One-Day projects

ROLE Participation

Evaluate and discuss your performance in a Results Only Learning Environment. Consider these topics:

- Collaboration—How well did you work collaboratively on a daily basis on both in-class activities and on projects?

- Self-discipline—In a class with no rules or consequences, how well did you manage your own conduct?

- Feedback—In a class that relies on narrative feedback about activities and projects, how well did you handle feedback? Did you provide feedback to the teacher? Did you use feedback to improve?

- Community—How did you contribute to our learning community? Did you help others grow?

(Continued)

7.2 | Performance Review (*Continued*)

Did peers look at you as someone who was a positive contributor?

Improvement

Evaluate and discuss what you need to improve, heading into high school. This is likely the most important part of this performance review. What goals should you set? How will you make sure that you follow through?

there were parts she didn't understand, I reviewed the guidelines for her specific project and implemented several changes to the instructions that will help future students.

By contrast, some students share amazing successes that validate particular projects. My top goal each year, for example, is that my students leave in June having read more than they ever had when they arrived in August. One of my all-time-favorite pieces of student feedback came when a student wrote in her year-end performance review that she never liked to read until she got the chance to pick her own books. Many students share particular parts of the class that helped them learn as well as parts they disliked. These student reviews help me shape my class each year.

8

Testing? No Problem

I had Mr. Barnes for two years. During the beginning of the first year, he told us about a new system called a Results Learning Only Environment (ROLE). I've grown to understand it now. The students have less stress about standardized testing because we don't have to keep cramming information in our heads. Instead, we have tons of different ways of learning that can make students want to learn more. In his class, we don't take a lot of tests; we take one or two for a whole year. I've learned that tests can't tell you how smart you are. In fact, when I take tests, sometimes I get nervous and don't do as well. Sometimes a very intelligent child doesn't do well on a test because he/she was having a bad day or accidently read the question wrong. Sometimes people bomb a test on purpose because they just "don't feel like" taking a test. So you never actually know how well you are doing just by taking a test. In Mr. Barnes' class, we use unique techniques to do well on tests. We do a lot of collaboration that helps us to learn new words. That way, when we are taking the achievement test, we know what the word means. In his class, students don't have to stress about a test coming up.

—Joanna Cha, 8th grade ROLE student

The two years before my conversion to results-only learning were not good standardized test years for my students. Only 74 percent of them passed the state-mandated Ohio Achievement Assessment (OAA). (Only 67 percent of "the bad bunch" passed.) Ironically, this was when most of my daily lessons included teaching to the test—using web-based tutorials, practice tests and quizzes, and OAA-style writing assignments, all structured to mirror Ohio's standardized test. Each day, I droned on and on about the test, as if it were the most important thing in our lives.

"Don't forget," I warned my students, "you have to pass this thing in 10th grade if you want to graduate." I was overcome by the delusion that the threat of not graduating in five years would throw my students into a frenzy of intense preparation for a high-stakes test they had absolutely no incentive to pass while attending middle school. In addition to bemoaning the importance of the yearly standardized test for all students, district administrators are even more passionate about getting minority students to pass. We are constantly reminded of the plethora of research that shows minorities, specifically African Americans, achieve at far lower rates than their Caucasian peers. (One can argue the reasons, but the evidence is hard to ignore.)

In those two years prior to the advent of a ROLE in my classes, just 64 percent of African American students in my classes passed the Ohio Achievement Assessment. Obviously, something was wrong, at least in terms of high-stakes test results, which have been proven to be ineffective methods for increasing student achievement (Bloomfield, 2011). However, since school districts are driven by state report cards that are based on these tests, I had to do something to improve the scores of all my students and help them become independent learners at the same time.

Enter results-only learning. Based on the exhaustive research I'd done in preparation for a ROLE, I felt much more passionate about my students building a strong thirst for learning than I did about test scores. "I know my scores haven't been good," I told a colleague early one school year, "but I feel a much bigger responsibility to just get my students to learn." Although at that time I didn't have any evidence to support my beliefs, I was certain that the results-only methods I intended to use would also help my students improve their standardized test scores. *They'll just become better learners,* I reasoned, *which will translate into being better test-takers.*

During my first year teaching in a ROLE, I eliminated all practice test activities and all online tutorial programs. I didn't speak in detail about the test until a couple of days prior to its arrival. Our administration mandates a practice run in December, so all students take a standardized test that is implemented exactly as the "real" one they will take in April. When the results come back, teachers are supposed to review them with students and dangle the scores over their heads for the next four months, like some sort of carrot or stick, depending on each student's performance on the practice test. I set the practice tests aside and never mentioned them to my students. Since I wasn't teaching to the test and my students still had plenty of work to complete on their year-long projects prior to the April test, the practice test scores had no perceptible value. Therefore, we forged ahead in a results-only style, and the achievement test came and went, like a thief in the night for my students. It was more like a havoc-wreaking tsunami for students in traditional classes, who had been peppered all year with practice test material and reminders of the repercussions of failure.

The Results

It would certainly make for a knight-in-shining-armor, fairy-tale ending if I could tell you that every single one of my students passed the achievement test that first year teaching in a ROLE and in all subsequent years. It didn't work out that way, though, and I'm not surprised. As I've alluded to throughout this book, the biggest problem with any test or quiz is that it evaluates a huge body of work in a very short amount of time, creating anxiety that often leads to rushed and careless responses.

Moreover, some students simply hate tests and see no value in them, so they "tank" the test on purpose—their way of rebelling against the system. Some students have told me they didn't try when I approached them the following year and expressed my surprise that they had failed. A guidance counselor at my school spends one meeting each school year regaling students with stories about many of their peers who were placed in remedial classes one year after failing the standardized reading test (despite the fact that they told her they didn't even try to do well on the test). This is one of the innumerable reasons I lend no credence to high-stakes tests. Still, standardized test results are important to state report cards and school administrators. If we're to sell a ROLE as revolutionary education reform, then it's important to review student scores if for no other reason than to compare them to scores of students who are rigorously prepared for the test with traditional methods—students who, in many cases, learn far less overall than their peers in a results-only classroom.

Even though I didn't achieve a 100 percent passing rate, the evidence supporting the success of a ROLE when it comes to standardized testing is overwhelming. In a system that abandoned all test-preparation practices, 84 percent of my students passed the Ohio Achievement Assessment the first year I used ROLE strategies—when I was still learning from my own mistakes. (87 percent of my students passed in my second year teaching in a ROLE.) This was better than all but one of my grade-level colleagues that first year, and her students passed at a rate of only about 1 percent higher than mine. It is worth noting that she had no students with learning disabilities, whereas 9 percent of my students had IEPs. Still, 56 percent of my students with learning disabilities passed the achievement test that first year. Each year, students with learning disabilities seem to flourish more in the results-only classroom.

Minority students in a ROLE also performed far better than in previous years. Indeed, 77 percent of African Americans in my classes passed the test, which was 13 percent more than the prior two years combined. Even more astounding is that 62 percent of all African American 7th graders at my school who failed the OAA my first year in the ROLE were taught in traditional classrooms, where much of the school year was spent on practice test activities. In my second year of results-only learning, when I was better at creating a community of self-directed learners, 84 percent of African American students in my classes passed the achievement test. These results clearly indicate that a student subgroup that has been one of the lowest-performing in my school and across my state on the standardized reading test is performing well in a Results Only Learning Environment.

One of the most remarkable statistics regarding ROLE students and achievement testing is the impact that results-only learning has on students who remain in a ROLE for consecutive years. Not long after I began teaching in a results-only classroom, I was moved from 7th to 8th grade. Thirty of my 105 students were returnees—students who had me as their language arts teacher in 7th grade. As the year progressed, I knew these students were flourishing. They read more than those who were my students for the first time. The returnees also handled feedback much better, making necessary changes to projects regularly. I assumed they would do well as a whole on the achievement test, but I was still surprised at how effective they were, knowing that many of them didn't typically perform well on multiple-choice tests. The numbers, though, were astonishing. Ninety-three percent of those students passed the test during their second year in a Results Only Learning Environment—most of them scoring in the top two tiers on the reading test. This, I believe, is one of the most profound aspects of the impact of results-only learning. When students are exposed for several years to a project-based learning community that deemphasizes grades and relies on autonomy and narrative feedback, they become independent learners and perform well on state-mandated tests.

What It Means

I have no interest in winding up on top of an achievement test numbers game, but these statistics present solid evidence of the effectiveness of results-only learning versus traditional teaching, which emphasizes test preparation, rote memory practice activities, and grades over project-based cooperative learning and narrative feedback. Feeling the pressure from upper administration to produce passing results, traditional teachers spend day after day and hour upon hour deciding how to apply state standards to in-class activities. Many teachers focus dozens of classes on test-taking strategies—a fruitless endeavor, in my opinion. Although many teachers believe that teaching students how to take a test helps them do well, there's very little empirical data to support this supposition. "Teaching to the test not only reduces the depth of instruction in specific subjects, but it also narrows the curriculum so that non-tested disciplines receive less attention during the school day" (Volante, 2004, para. 9).

During the two years prior to creating a ROLE, I labored feverishly on test-taking strategies with my students only to see 26 percent of them fail the test. Not only were they not developing a thirst for learning during engaging and collaborative year-long projects, they were also not passing what administrators believe to be the lightning rod of education—the high-stakes test. After I eliminated all traditional methods and test-taking strategies, crafting a learning environment that creates students who want to demonstrate excellence, less than 14 percent of my students failed the test. It's worth noting that more than half of those who failed missed passing by four points—the equivalent of one question.

The central point here is that students in a Results Only Learning Environment perform at least as well (if not better) on standardized tests as their peers in traditional classes. What's most important, however, is not the correlation between results-only strategies and test achievement; rather, it is that students in a ROLE learn far more than students in traditional classes and still perform equally well on standard-ized tests. A results-only classroom presents the best of both worlds—real learning coupled with the test results that district administrators covet. Real learning has no longer to fall victim to test preparation. The Results Only Learning Environment has proven this.

9

Disciplining Students?
Forget About It

On day one, when I walked into my Language Arts class, I thought it was going to be another long year of being forced to read boring books on the assigned book list, grammar assignments out of the workbooks, and tons of homework. To my surprise, it was a fun atmosphere where students could interact with each other. Yes, believe it or not, we could talk in class. Not only could we talk, we got to use our cell phones and computers too. We got immediate feedback from the teacher about the class activities, on his website that he set up for his Language Arts classes. Imagine that, everyone had their own web page. Coming to class was exciting, and this wasn't going to be just another ordinary year!

—Cameron Ford, 8th grade ROLE student

Most teachers are far too quick to judge their students based on their prior records or what others say about them. Think back for a moment to when you've had a former student's sibling a year or two later. Maybe his or her predecessor disrupted the class on numerous occasions. On the first day of class, you might have said something like, "Oh, you're Jackie's little sister, huh? Well, I'm definitely going to keep an eye on you." Even if you said it with tongue in cheek, you inadvertently set the tone for a poor relationship. I used to be this way—a classic judge.

I assumed a particular group of students would be disrespectful and disruptive because colleagues told me they would be. I treated them as poorly behaved students from the beginning, and, of course, that's what they became. Rules and consequences were my crutches. Students were disruptive mainly because they were bored with the worksheets I kept putting in front of them. In an attempt to control the disruptors, I threw rules at them. You know the kind. They were likely similar to those posted around your school or classroom, each one more ridiculous than the last:

1. No chewing gum.
2. No bathroom breaks.
3. No talking.
4. No food or drink in the classroom.
5. No leaving your seat.
6. No holes in your jeans.
7. No being tardy.
8. No cell phones.
9. (Insert other ridiculous rule here.)

Let us not forget the accompanying punishments for breaking these rules: name on the board, timeout, a new seat assignment, detention, an old-fashioned tongue-lashing, or the abundantly popular office referral (i.e., shipping the problem child off to a principal).

There is certainly no shortage of classroom management books and papers that outline the "proper methods" for disciplining children and maintaining order in a classroom. Some advocate endless structure, including the aforementioned list of rules and punishments posted ominously in the classroom for all would-be miscreants to see. Others prefer the soft touch of assertive discipline, which, among other bizarre practices, invites students to create their own classroom rules. Of course, it doesn't take long to figure out this really just amounts to teachers guiding their students to create the rules that they themselves want, which sounds a lot like trickery to me.

In Chapter 1, I shared the story of how I tell students on the first day of school that we have no rules. Subsequent chapters demonstrate how a workshop setting, cooperative groups, and narrative feedback help maintain a classroom with little or no behavior issues. In this chapter, I'd like to make some additional connections between ROLE strategies and behavior. As you read these techniques, keep in mind that the success of a results-only classroom is part of a complete recipe (see Figure 9.1). One concept works because of the others, and student behavior is no different. Once students see that you believe in the system and will remain true to it, they will believe too. However, this will only happen with the elimination of control. If you say there are no rules, then you can't create one a few weeks later because it might seem convenient. You can't trumpet an environment with no consequences and then move a child's seat at the first sign of trouble. If you tell students they can leave your classroom when they need to without explanation, then you can't back down the first time a student goes to the bathroom two or three times in one week.

To eliminate the control that deconstructs traditional classrooms, the ROLE teacher must make choice a part of everything, including most of the decisions students make. "Children are not just adults-in-the-making. They are people whose current needs and rights and experiences must be taken seriously" (Kohn, 2006a, p. 81). No one tells you when you may go to the bathroom or when to get a drink of water during the school day, yet teachers readily tell their students when they can and cannot perform these basic human needs. When your students see you take their rights and experiences seriously, they will appreciate you, and this appreciation will be accompanied by respect for you and the classroom.

9.1 | Five ROLE Strategies for Creating a Problem-Free Classroom

1. **Throw out all rules.** Never post "Do and Don't" signs in your room, as these are about control. Instead of rules or classroom guidelines, discuss mutual respect with your students. Tell students from day one that you trust them to make the right decisions. They will be amazed, because you will likely be the first teacher who has said this to them.

2. **Replace control with freedom.** Ignore the insignificant rules that most schools have, and give students real autonomy. When students want to use the restroom or return to their lockers, let them. Never assign point values to basic human needs. Never admonish students for coming late. Instead, emphasize that their peers in a cooperative environment depend on them. Let students choose some learning activities and some collaborative groups. Freedom is the guideline here. Students value it.

3. **Never punish.** ROLE teachers simply do not give consequences, and as hard as this may be to comprehend, once you eliminate them, even the most difficult students will begin to behave. Rather than punish a student, it's always better to talk to him or her one-on-one and explore the problem and its solution together.

4. **Build rapport.** Everything you do either builds or burns bridges with your students. It took me roughly 16 years to learn this but only one to see how absolutely true it is. Sarcasm and yelling are never acceptable under any circumstance. What you think is a harmless joke may irreparably damage your relationship with a student. Emphasize that all students are a valuable part of your learning community. When you show students that you care about them, they will like you. I used to think this wasn't important. Now, when students see that the only thing I care about is their well-being and that they develop a thirst for learning, they abandon disruption for cooperation.

5. **Emphasize results-only learning.** In addition to year-long projects, narrative feedback, and the elimination of all other traditional teaching methods, what really creates a thirst for learning is intrinsic motivation. This constant emphasis of a ROLE will help fan the intrinsic motivation that already exists within students, and the more they understand this, the more they will embrace learning and lose interest in disruption.

Homework and Class Disruption

Not only is homework rarely connected to academic achievement, it is also damaging to grades (if you are, in fact, grading it). It's been my experience that many students who are disruptive in class are also those who do not complete homework assignments. A class with no homework eliminates pressure and abolishes a practice that lowers many students' grades. If you don't have to chase down students for unfinished homework and if you stop calling parents to complain about missing assignments, then you will begin to build bridges rather than tear them down. On the other hand, harassing students for homework and threatening punishment via grades or other methods creates tension between you and the student, leading to the sort of discordant relationship that may ultimately entice that student to be disruptive in class.

Consider any time in your career when you may have called a parent because of a student's ongoing failure to complete homework assignments. You explained that the child's grade was suffering and he may be facing summer school or, worse, retention. In most cases, this particular child was headed for a confrontation at home and maybe even some nasty consequences. Who is to blame for the student's hardship? As a reasonable adult guided by logic, you may say the child put himself in that predicament. Of course, he didn't feel this way. He probably blamed you.

Returning to my earlier point—that ROLE strategies are intertwined—it should be evident that homework, which has negligible effects on achievement, can have a profound impact on student-teacher rapport. And this is what ultimately leads to problems in class. It's certainly reasonable to believe that if a student blames you for his fate at home, he will be less-than-motivated to work for you in class. More likely, he will be eager to disrupt class as payback for getting him into trouble.

Collaboration Breeds Cooperation

You may recall that I was afraid to put "the bad bunch" in small groups. I felt they were just too out of control to handle cooperative learning. Little did I realize that cooperative learning was exactly what they needed. I was so busy trying to control them that I didn't realize giving up control would have settled them. This goes back to what I call "good chaos." When your students talk, share, swap materials, or leave their seats, they feel less constrained. My students are in groups all year long. I change their groups often, trying to get them to work with as many of their peers as possible. I challenge them to get to know one another's strengths and weaknesses and to value the progress of all individuals in the group. Allowing students to solve the conflicts that invariably arise is another pivotal part of group work in a ROLE. Kohn explains this best: "To discourage (let alone punish) objections is to sacrifice the development of judgment to the imperative of conformity" (2006a, p. 76). Most important, I want each class to build a learning community with similar goals. Recall for a moment the discovery activity on literary terms. There are so many cooperative fabrics and opportunities for learning associated with this activity that disruption is never a consideration. All students have a role in activities such as this. A well-planned cooperative lesson will engage any student.

Learning Communities Decategorize Students

In decades as a public school teacher, I've found that students considered to be behavior problems fall into only three categories:

- Those who need attention.
- Those with anger-management issues (and possibly emotional problems).
- Those who are bored or distracted (either because they're not challenged or because they have a personal issue unrelated to class).

Although I don't think these are new labels, I believe that any student who willingly disrupts class fits into one of these categories. Students with anger-management issues can be the most difficult because they may have psychological or emotional problems that the average teacher often isn't equipped to handle. Bored and distracted students are the easiest to engage in a ROLE, although the more difficult attention-seekers and angry students can also be pulled into learning in a ROLE's collaborative environment. A community of learners can decategorize any student when a skilled ROLE teacher acts as a classroom facilitator. The key is getting all students to see the value of collaboration. A well-designed cooperative activity can engage students on a variety of levels and help them taste the kind of academic success they might rarely experience. A student who needs attention can get plenty of it in the right group setting. Most attention-seekers have leadership qualities precisely because they have been "showing off" in front of peers for many years. I always attempt to put these students in a leadership role in small groups. Students with anger problems can be set off by a myriad of seemingly insignificant things. The results-only classroom and the workshop setting eliminate many of these potential issues.

A ROLE is a vibrant, fast-paced classroom that presents students with learning opportunities that engage even the most ardent disrupters. Potentially difficult students find the attention they need, something to dissipate their anger, or something to break their boredom. When students who are typically labeled as disruptive become part of the learning community that a ROLE creates, their need for attention, their angry outbursts, or their distraction is typically eliminated. When students feel important, they want to collaborate. Soon, collaboration will become second nature, and formerly disruptive students will be interested in learning for learning's sake.

Goodbye to Control

"Teachers tend to have 'control' issues of their classroom. We have a paradigm of what teaching looks like. This paradigm usually includes the teacher in the front 'teaching' students who are at their seats" (Jenkins, 2011). Without turning this into another book on classroom management, I want to clearly illustrate how I gave up the kind of control Jenkins describes and what I've replaced it with. For a moment, consider the rules and consequences listed at the beginning of this chapter. I used to live by these. In the my-way-or-the-highway days, a student caught chewing gum more than once was asked to come after school and clean gum off desks—a revolting punishment that I stood firmly behind, even when challenged one time by an angry parent. Wearing pants with holes in the knees was grounds for dismissal to our student management room. If a cell phone rang, it was immediately taken and turned into the office. Disruptive students were shouted at and told to see the principal. Notes were sent home, parents were called, and formal referrals were written and placed in permanent records.

Today, I have no rules, and I don't raise my voice. Students chew gum if they like, wear jeans with holes, and use cell phones and iPods regularly. My bathroom policy is simple: students go when the need arises. I talk to those who leave too frequently and explain the value of being in class. "I don't want you to miss any important discussions, reading, or time you might be working on a project," I say. "Remember, your group members are counting on you." The key is emphasizing the value of class, not admonishing a kid who may legitimately be answering nature's call. Forcing students to ask for permission for natural acts such as going to the bathroom or getting a drink of water is a further demonstration of teacher control. Teachers who enforce these rules are seen as authority figures rather than as facilitators of learning. If you suggest that you want students to have autonomy, yet you enforce insignificant rules and policies, then you risk undermining the freedom you say you want students to have in a results-only classroom.

Consider the power of *not* enforcing silly rules when it comes to creating a comfortable learning environment. The majority of my students spend three-quarters of their school day being told *no* or *don't* by adults. No gum, no candy, no cell phones, no torn jeans, and no leaving your seat. Don't go to the bathroom, don't talk to your friends, and don't you dare walk in without a pencil. Then they come to a results-only classroom and are met with an uncanny amount of freedom. You might think they race in and start blowing bubbles, jumping up and down, shouting, and sending text messages by the dozens, but it is quite the contrary. There is a remarkable respect for a ROLE. Since I've spent so much time coaching intrinsic motivation, cooperative learning, and community building, my students buy in. Believe it or not, almost all of them just want to do things right.

Constant Communication

A results-only classroom is built around feedback, which is constant two-way communication between teacher and student. In the past, communication with students whom I considered to be disciplinary problems consisted of incessant redirection or threats of consequence for some insignificant rule they were breaking. If I had a sidebar, the intent was to admonish the student or notify him or her of an impending punishment such as a seat change or referral to a principal. I wasn't a complete ogre; I'd still attempt to engage disruptive students in class activities and encourage them to do their work. These overtures, though, always came with ultimatums. "I need you to do some work, or I'll have to recommend you for summer school," I might say. Sometimes I'd call attention to a typically disruptive student who was sitting quietly for a moment, which only served to embarrass him or her in front of his peers. "What's the difference between today and any other day?" I'd ask. The student wondered what I meant. "Normally, you're shouting across the room or making some smart-aleck comment, but today you're quiet." This usually made the attention-seeker want to return to old habits, if only to impress his friends who likely thought I had showed him up.

In a ROLE, the communication is always constructive, positive, and friendly. When I'm not giving written or verbal feedback about projects and class activities, I'm using sidebars to build rapport with my students. I try to speak to every student in every class several times each week. This can be challenging, especially in larger classes, but the workshop setting helps me get to know students very well. I listen to them and attempt to join their conversations. Asking about their plans for the weekend, inquiring about a presentation for another class, or asking about struggles in science or math class builds bridges. By showing students you care more about their welfare than whether they are chewing gum or came to class 30 seconds late, you build a rapport that creates lasting mutual respect.

"No matter the method, developing personal relationships with students is a win-win. You have the chance to be a role model and personally influence the young people in your class in a positive manner that helps raise their self-esteem" (Kuntz, 2011, p. 8). This kind of communication can also work with the whole group in order to give students a sense of ownership in the environment directly responsible for their learning. When Pernille Ripp converted to results-only learning, she moved to a workshop setting and most discipline problems vanished. It was a difficult transition, at first, as Ripp explains: "If the whole class or a majority of students were off [task], we had a class meeting. . . . The kids got used to it and many of them relished the fact that they were given a voice in their behavior and how to fix it, rather than a dictation from me" (Ripp, 2011a, para. 4). Individual sidebars and whole-group communication completely change the climate of a results-only classroom.

A Magical Transformation

The transformation in student behavior that has occurred in my classroom is so remarkable that it's the one thing about a ROLE that I have difficulty pinpointing for people. During my worst year of teaching, just before I started a results-only classroom, I estimate that I handed out more than 500 punishments of some kind. That's nearly three consequences per day. Now, every year, the punishment number is virtually zero. There is simply no need for consequences. When major problems arise, we talk it out, sometimes a parent or an administrator is brought in, and we create a plan for success. There are occasions when a student is so upset about something that outbursts occur. When this happens, I simply ask the student to leave the room for a "cooling down" period (sometimes, he or she is sent to a colleague's room); then I speak to the student privately, and he or she quietly returns. Other times, we just step into the hallway, and I talk to the student immediately. People have told me this is hard to believe. Remember, the ultimate recipe for a trouble-free classroom is ROLE strategies combined with the elimination of control. This combination creates an almost magical environment.

The magic, I believe, lies within the system as a whole. My success with behavior and engagement does not rely on any single element. It is the symbiotic relationship of everything discussed in this book. It's teaching methods that get students excited about learning—choice, collaboration, online instruction, and year-long projects. It's the end of grades, which serve in most cases only to pressure and punish students. It's narrative feedback, both written and verbal, which creates constant two-way communication between teacher and student. It's the total elimination of nonsensical rules and even stranger consequences. It's the creation of a classroom built on collaboration and a thirst for learning. A Results Only Learning Environment is a remarkable system that surprises and thrills students so much that even the thought of disrespect or disruption disappears forever.

Joining the Movement: Transform Your School

Wisdom is not a product of schooling but of the lifelong attempt to acquire it.

—*Albert Einstein*

When my experiment with a ROLE began, I wasn't interested in changing teachers at my school; in fact, it was quite the opposite. What I wanted to do was reinvent myself as a teacher, and I was nervous but excited about doing it. There was no guarantee that the changes I had prepared would work out as planned. There were rampant concerns about how students, parents, and administrators would react to a system that gives learners choice and freedom while completely eliminating traditional teaching methods and grades. Most of all, I lay awake many nights and wondered if this radical change would actually make my students better.

Initially, I was not overly enthusiastic about sharing what I was doing with my peers. I kept most of my strategies pretty quiet at first. In fact, I only told my principal when interim grades were due for our first marking period. She printed the report cards that were generated by all teachers, using our online grade program, and mine were the only ones without letter grades. I was surprised when she interrupted my class one day, holding printouts of interim reports. "Your grades aren't in," she whispered, while my students continued with their project work, ignoring our conversation (by this time, they were used to the bustle that occurs almost daily in our workshop setting). I whispered back, somewhat sheepishly, that I wasn't grading my students. I explained there was a simple "satisfactory progress" comment on the interim report. She would be filled in later, I promised.

As you can see, I didn't parade around the hallways of my school that year shouting, "Hey, everyone, let's turn our school into a Results Only Learning Environment." It wasn't until the second grading period that I started leaking information about what I was doing and how it impacted my students. Word began to spread, and questions poured in about results-only learning. If this were fiction, I'd share a story about how my school amazingly morphed into a progressive place with student-centered practices implemented schoolwide. This wasn't the case, though. When ideas for this book began hitting my journal, few people even knew what a ROLE was, but the principal was on board, and teachers started to listen with curiosity when I would talk about the successes my students were experiencing in this new style of teaching and learning. As the second semester moved forward, I began ROLEizing my school, whether my colleagues knew it or not.

I shared success stories with anyone who would listen. When discussions about discipline crept into our grade-level meetings, I considered it a wonderful opportunity to pontificate on how eliminating rules and consequences would bring order to chaos. At department meetings, I was constantly trying to work my Reading All Year project into the discussion, goading my colleagues to create similar activities. I began to realize that if results-only learning were to become a reality in classrooms nationwide, teachers everywhere would have to give it a voice.

From that point on, I talked about the ROLE. I shared articles and research with colleagues about student-centered classes and no-homework practices. I tweeted about results-only learning and shared presentations online and at major education conferences. Soon, teachers began contacting me, sharing their own stories about the progressive classes they had created and how they had adopted aspects of results-only learning. Eventually, teachers from around the country (and even outside of it) began sharing ROLE stories and calling their classrooms Results Only Learning Environments. A movement was beginning.

The ROLE Is Spreading

Joey Till is a teacher at a middle school in northern Indiana. Till discovered results-only learning early in the 2011 school year while reading my blog, *ROLE Reversal*. His story is similar to mine—he'd taught for a long time and was feeling unsuccessful. He needed a change, so he contacted me with questions about results-only learning, and soon after he was steaming toward his own teaching change. "I always thought there was a better way," Till told me, "I just didn't know how to get there." Our correspondence continued for a few weeks, and Till questioned me about narrative feedback, project-based assessment, and getting students to buy in to the process. He also shared an array of successes he'd experienced early on in his new Results Only Learning Environment.

Unlike me, Till could not keep his early enthusiasm about teaching in a ROLE to himself. Enter Justin Vail, a social studies teacher who works down the hall from Till. Since Vail was already using project-based learning and other progressive teaching methods, he was open-minded when Till approached him about experimenting with results-only learning. Less than one month after Till recruited Vail to start a ROLE of his own, the three of us were sharing our experiences during a Skype video conference. It wasn't long before Vail began his own steady stream of observations about successfully converting his classroom into a Results Only Learning Environment. "The self-evaluation process is difficult for some kids. I sometimes have to prod the students to express themselves, but eventually they are very honest about their work and their work ethic. In fact, students are often harder on themselves than I would be. I have evaluated nearly 200 projects this year, and less than five times have students suggested a 'grade' higher than what I thought" (Vail, 2011, para. 4).

As you can see, finding a colleague to join you in ROLEizing your classroom should help ease the difficulties that accompany the transition. This kinship, along with the information I've provided so far about how the system works, should be enough to help you be the voice that ultimately converts your school into a Results Only Learning Environment. The system is simple, but the transition may be slow and methodical. This chapter provides a blueprint for turning your school into a ROLE. Understand that this is not an all-encompassing design; there may be steps that are more appropriate for one school than another. This should be a group effort, and you may want to consider using a team of people to put your own plan in place and take on this imposing challenge of education reform.

Blueprint for Change

Start Small

Until more schools nationwide begin using some sort of a results-only system, it will be difficult for teachers or principals to begin the school year by announcing sweeping changes in classroom methods and school rules. A better start would be to give an overview of a ROLE to your staff and have a small team of teachers begin initiating the system. This might take a whole school year. Periodically, the test teacher or team should report back to the faculty on the success of the system. Comprehensive reports on implementing the system should be written, and other helpful teaching tools, such as videos of the results-only class in action, should be provided. These will help skeptical teachers with their own transition to a ROLE. By the second half of the school year, other teachers may be bold enough to begin converting their own classrooms.

Commit to One New Schoolwide Strategy

As noted earlier, my results-only classroom was not widely publicized at first. With such a dramatic change in teaching methods, evaluation, grading, and classroom management, I was reluctant to share my experiment out of fear that I would be told not to pursue it. I envisioned a principal or upper administrator saying, "Oh, no, you can't stop grading papers." Worse yet, someone might ask, "How will your students pass the achievement test if you don't use practice worksheets?" Using advice a colleague shared when I was a new teacher, I decided to just go with my gut and apologize later if things didn't work out. If I had prior experience or research—such as this book, for example—I would have done things differently. Most likely, I would have shared my plan with administration before the school year even began. I would have said, "Hey, after plenty of research and lots of consideration, I've decided to make some changes in how I do things this year." I advise any teacher reading this book to do the same.

Having said this, I believe it's important to do everything you can to get your entire staff to commit to one ROLE-type strategy. This is a subtle way to begin a schoolwide transition to a ROLE. A persuasive principal who believes in what's best for all students should be willing to make this happen, especially if you've carefully explained your plan. A few years before I converted to a ROLE, I spoke to my principal about having teachers cut back on the amount of homework they assign. I had already begun phasing out homework in my own classes because it was killing my students' grades. I gave the principal plenty of research on the subject, and we discussed ways to get other teachers to see its deleterious effects. He began sharing his thoughts about the negative impact of homework with the staff, and I did all I could to speak out against it too. The principal even put together a small committee of teachers to investigate a new homework policy for my school, and I cochaired this committee. Although the effort started too late and no new policy was created, many teachers assigned less homework as a result. Some even eliminated homework completely.

Consider the ROLE strategies outlined in this book and which one your staff might be willing to adopt. The principal might tell faculty at the beginning of the year that a few basic handbook rules are being discarded. The principal might say he or she wants every teacher to create a year-long project that incorporates a wide variety of learning outcomes. (This is easy to do if you teach in teams; you can prepare an interdisciplinary project together.) Perhaps homework is to be cut back or eliminated, at least for one marking period. If all teachers agree to embrace at least one of these strategies, then you'll be on your way to converting the school into a Results Only Learning Environment.

Get Parent Support

I typically have a packed room during our annual open house and first set of parent-teacher conferences. Parents are eager to learn more about the unique teaching strategies I use, why there's no homework, and how a class with no grades works. These meetings are critical since I want to forge good relationships with parents and because I want them to understand and value the results-only system. Every time you talk to parents, even if it's just bumping into them at school functions, be sure to talk up how their children are flourishing in your results-only class-room. Emphasize the year-long projects you are using and how invested your students are in their own learning. It may seem like salesmanship, but in a way, all teachers have to sell what they do to parents. You are selling much more than one system. You're selling education reform.

You'd be surprised at how far a few well-placed phone calls or e-mails can go in getting parents to buy into results-only learning. I respond to every parent e-mail the same day I receive it. If the content is about a student's grade, then I talk up narrative feedback and self-evaluation. If it's about a class activity, then I discuss the value of our year-long projects. When classroom management issues arise, I outline the many freedoms my students have in our workshop and collaborative settings. It's ROLE strategies all the time, and parents are soon passing along the positives of results-only learning to their peers and my administrators. Near the end of the school year, I have had intervention specialists, who are transitioning students from elementary school to my building, tell me that their students' parents have asked for their children to be placed in my class because of the remarkable methods I use. Some like the technology, many covet the feedback, and others love the freedom. Parents with special-needs children believe they will flourish in an environment where students are not required to be nailed to their seats. There have even been parents who told me they heard about my methods from a neighbor with a child in my class, and they wanted their child to have a similar experience. I am quick to tell them that it is not about me (there are, in fact, many teachers who are more nurturing and quick-witted than I, whom students love). Whether they realize it or not, it's the ROLE students want, but parent communication is always important.

Follow Through

Assuming your principal agrees to implement at least some elements of a ROLE schoolwide, staff training will be necessary. As the school's catalyst for results-only learning, you may need to teach others how to build a ROLE of their own. This can be done in several ways. The easiest way would be to bring an expert in to help with the transition; a day or two of professional development could help teachers begin changing their methods. If your school can't afford this type of training, then it can be done at faculty meetings where you share your own strategies. You can always refer to this book as a blueprint. A few

30-minute question-and-answer sessions will also ease the tension about major reform. Maybe your principal will agree to let you go around your building and observe teachers who ask for assistance. You can monitor how they are transitioning and offer suggestions for creating a better workshop setting, eliminating rules and consequences, coaching students on the system, or supplying meaningful feedback. This sort of follow-through will be critical if an entire school is to take on this kind of major reform.

After my rookie year as a ROLE teacher, I felt supremely confident. I believed every day would be a success. Nothing could go wrong now that I was a ROLE expert. Then, one day, a student shouted an obscenity-laced threat my way, and that was it; the dam had burst. She was unceremoniously dismissed from class, and my problem-free workshop setting was destroyed. At least that's what I thought for a fleeting moment. It was disconcerting that I had jettisoned a student from our ROLE, a place devoid of rules and consequences, to the student management room—a move I hadn't made in what seemed like forever. Suddenly, I felt like a failure. That night, as I reflected on the day and that event, I realized it was just one minor blemish on an otherwise beautiful model. A little plastic surgery, though, was necessary. The next day, the student returned, and I spoke to her. I hadn't followed up with an office referral, which would carry a severe punishment, and I wanted to discuss what happened and start fresh. She explained what caused her outburst and apologized. Things quickly returned to normal. I realized that one of the keys to a successful ROLE is to always work the program. It may sound colloquial, but I can't overemphasize the value of perseverance in a results-only system.

Although my first two years in a ROLE brought a myriad of victories, there were more than a handful of times I considered abandoning results-only learning entirely. 'Maybe they can't handle choice,' I thought when a few students struggled on projects. When a student felt she deserved an *A* despite underperforming, my first thought was 'Perhaps I should go back to putting numbers on their papers and letting the math take care of the grade.' If a few students abused our laid-back hall pass plan, I was quick to question the program and students' ability to handle self-discipline. These moments of self-doubt were critical to my own growth as the facilitator of a Results Only Learning Environment. The answer to almost every issue was always an easy one: work the program.

Like other parts of teaching, you have to take the good with the bad. Results-only learning is a powerful system that can improve education around the world. Still, it's not perfect. There will be many wonderful days, but there will be a few bad ones sprinkled in. Never let the few bad days or poor student decisions make you to doubt a ROLE. Your students are still kids, and they are subject to poor judgment, no matter how hard you coach them on decision making. Just keep working the plan. This may mean pulling a student aside and reminding him or her about the intrinsic motivation that is so important to your class or how year-long projects demonstrate real learning. Use the term *results-only learning* often, and always explain what it means or, better yet, have a student explain it. Remind your students they are in a classroom that is driven by collaboration and autonomy. How they work with one another and the choices they make are critical to everyone's success or failure. Tell students daily, if possible, that your class is about production, feedback, and change. They don't receive number or letter grades because those don't help them learn. Remind students that you always want what is best for them. It's about trial–error–improvement–mastery, not trial–failure–move on. Try to have a sidebar with every student at least once a week—even if it's a simple question such as "What did you do over the weekend?" or "How did your history project go?" This type of communication is crucial to building the rapport that will make your ROLE run without disruption. Never stop working the program. Keep reminding yourself and your students that it works.

Getting Help

Before I could coach my students and their parents on the virtues of a results-only classroom, I had to solve many of my own problems, and it didn't take long to realize I would need help. At first, most of my colleagues didn't know what I was doing. Still, this didn't mean they couldn't be instrumental in decisions that would impact the functionality of my results-only classroom. When I was deciding on ways to communicate narrative feedback to both students and their parents, I knew our online grade book would be a central piece, but I wasn't sure how. After all, I didn't want a letter grade to show up for my students. If I used numbers or even indications of completed or missing activities, then the program defaulted to some kind of percentage and corresponding letter grade. When I checked "missing" for an activity or project, the student appeared to be getting an *F*. I was stumped, so I sought out the help of a colleague. Without explaining the complete transformation I was making, I told her I wanted to supply narrative feedback rather than numbers and letters, but our grade book wasn't cooperating. A fresh mind was just what I needed, since she knew how to handle it so I could place feedback only without a grade or percentage.

Converting the classroom into a workshop setting and creating engaging year-long projects with substantial student choice are important aspects of a ROLE's success, so I knew I also needed help here. I was constantly visiting other classrooms, looking for ideas I could use to make my room more workshop friendly. I needed ideas to build choice and creativity into my year-long reading project. Our school's library media specialist, Lisa, was immensely helpful to me in this area. She had suggestions for popular books, means of demonstrating understanding, ways to get students to embrace reading, and numerous online resources that made the project more educational and fun. During that first year, I often found myself looking for excuses to stop by the media center's circulation desk, when all I really wanted to do was tell Lisa something new I was trying and get her feedback.

A very special group of colleagues played a significant role as my sounding board—a necessary tool for any teacher making major changes to a classroom and teaching style. Over lunch in the faculty lounge, these amazing teachers listened intently to the ROLE strategies I was employing. They offered support and inquiry, and I needed both. Playing the roles of parents and senior administrators, they would ask questions such as, "What will you tell parents who want to see scores and grades on all activities?" "How do you know if they've mastered all of the standards if you aren't giving unit tests?" "What will you say to an administrator who questions what you're doing?"

These were legitimate questions that gave me plenty to ponder. This group's contribution to my success can't be overlooked. When my school transitioned to academic teams, a very special group of colleagues also kept me going, during particularly difficult times. Early one school year, our team of 7th and 8th graders was struggling to adapt to our system. Although my colleagues hadn't yet made a full transition to ROLE strategies, they were using some, so it was easy to collaborate on key decisions that helped our students adjust to more autonomy and less teacher control. When you make your own transition to a results-only classroom, you will need colleagues as both shoulders to cry on and as voices of constructive criticism. Remember, you can't make this sort of transformation on your own, so be sure to get some help.

Repetition, Repetition, Repetition

Year-long projects reinforce the skills and critical thinking practices that are paramount to any class. My students' reading comprehension levels increase dramatically throughout the year, and their vocabulary acquisition is uncanny—not because I'm a great teacher but because the constant reading, mixed with minilessons about structure, genre, and literary elements, does most of the work. Consider a results-only system like one of your well-crafted year-long projects. The built-in components of the system will help your students grow and learn, but you will constantly have to remind them that these pieces exist and about the purpose of each element. For example, you can't teach intrinsic motivation at the beginning of the year and never mention it again. I use the term often and mix in use of the term *Type I*. Early in the year, I share excerpts from a YouTube video that is based on Daniel Pink's concepts of autonomy, mastery, and purpose and how they are driven by intrinsic motivation (RSA Animate, 2010). I explain to students that Type I people are driven by intrinsic motivation—that they want to achieve for the sake of achieving. When we're working in small groups and students take the activity to the next level, I'll point it out to the class and say something like, "This is that Type I learning we talk so much about." Type I learners, I remind them, are those who are self-directed and want to learn for learning's sake.

Once a month, I like to revisit the concepts behind a Results Only Learning Environment with my students. A brief conversation about how we do things versus how they are done in other classes is useful for illuminating the value of results-only learning. I'm always careful with comparisons. I never mention other teachers by name, and I never openly vilify the methods of my colleagues. The discussion invariably focuses on how learning is different in a ROLE. I want my students to know that grades are not important and they will always benefit from narrative feedback. Their autonomy is of critical importance. I remind them that self-evaluation is a remarkable tool they must always work on sharpening. The key is repetition. A successful ROLE and its parts must be discussed often.

ROLEing with Parents

Most honest teachers will admit they rarely want to talk to parents. Due to the unknowns that surround the encounters, there is usually an ominous fear hovering over phone calls or meetings with parents. My first year of teaching in a ROLE was rife with interesting parent conversations and e-mails. You see, we weren't just discussing the students that year; in fact, much of our communication was about results-only learning. Like other stakeholders, parents are accustomed to classrooms looking the same, and when some upstart teacher strays from the norm, things can get dicey. Here is a typical e-mail you may encounter in a ROLE, if you handle report card grades as I do: "Ricky will be meeting with a tutor on Mondays, and any insight you can give about his strengths and weaknesses (areas of improvement) in English would be greatly appreciated. What caused his grade to go from an *A* to a *B+* in quarter 2?"

This is certainly an innocuous letter, but the potential for it to turn sour is present. Ricky's mother wants my opinion, which I'm thrilled to provide. Here is how I responded:

> Regarding Ricky's grade, you should ask him about it. My class is built on a foundation of results only, which means students produce school activities, get written feedback from me, and make changes that I recommend; we do not live in the points-and-percentages world in my class. With no points or percentages to make up a final grade, my students grade themselves at the end of each quarter, based on a thorough self-evaluation of their production and my feedback. Ricky "gave" himself an *A–*, which we don't have at our school, so we settled on *B+*.
>
> I have encouraged my students to focus more on learning and less on letter grades, as research indicates that grades only bring out the worst in students. So-called *A* students work less and often cheat, whereas *D/F* students grow to hate school. We're currently working on a reading workshop in which students are selecting novels by genre. We're doing a lot of reading in class, but since I'm asking students to complete 10 books by the end of the semester, I recommend a lot of reading outside of school and during "down time" within the school day. This will help Ricky in all areas of language arts, as reading is the best teacher.

Ricky's mother responded with gratitude, and we arranged a later meeting. That meeting went remarkably well, and Ricky's father commented that he loved how we do things in our class. There have been many e-mail messages since I changed the way I teach. As parents aren't present daily to see a ROLE in action and hear the constant support for its components, it typically takes them much longer to understand the system fully. Constant feedback on your online grade book, on your classroom website, and through e-mails and phone calls will ease most tensions about results-only learning.

There may be times of frustration; some parents will ring the grade bell relentlessly. You have to remember that, like students and most teachers, parents have been conditioned to believe that school and grades go together. Reform takes time. I remind parents at every opportunity that homework and grades are negative parts of school and do not improve academic achievement. At our open houses and parent-teacher conferences, I distribute copies of research-based articles about the ineffectiveness of both homework and grades. I always have these articles lying around or placed on a table outside my room for parents waiting to see me at conferences.

You Can't Fight City Hall, or Can You?

Many of my colleagues are still skeptical about my move to results-only learning. The biggest issue in most cases isn't a fear of failure or even that students might revolt if given too much freedom. What scares them most is the punishment they believe awaits when administrators discover they've traded in their curriculum guides for something far more educational. When I moved to a Results Only Learning Environment, there simply wasn't room for much of what some administrators believe should be taught. If I spent eight weeks teaching short stories from a decades-old textbook, then I'd have to give up time that is dedicated to my year-long projects. If every student labored over a lengthy research paper, citing sources like an attorney citing case law for a 50-page brief, then any credibility I had with my students would be lost. Instead, my students collaborate on research, citing only a few sources on topics they select, and they use that research as a starting point for our Make a Difference project. They post short papers to online libraries, and they don't hate the unit as past students have.

Spending six weeks reading a class novel and discussing each page until it yellows with age erodes the autonomy of a ROLE. We share one short novel at the beginning of the year, and then my students choose their own books to read independently all year, even though this isn't exactly what the course of study mandates. "But what will you say if an administrator asks you why you don't stick to the curriculum?" a colleague once asked. I explained that no matter what their education philosophy is, most administrators realize that schools and students are measured by their standardized test scores. I'll tell any administrator who is curious about a ROLE that "Most of my students will pass the test. Plus, they'll read and write more efficiently than ever." (Nearly 90 percent of my students score at or above grade level in vocabulary.)

I can't imagine any school leader who would prefer I teach in a traditional fashion and have my students fail the test when I can teach in a ROLE and get most of them to pass. One of the rewards of teaching in a results-only classroom is knowing that as irrelevant as high-stakes testing is to learning, students will still pass standardized tests when they are in a ROLE. Plus, they become better learners.

Remember, you can replace parts of your curriculum with more effective workshop-style activities and year-long projects, and you will not lose any learning. Even if you skip days of practice and direct instruction on some of your state standards, your well-designed project will cover them in most cases. You can abandon homework and other activities that purportedly prepare students for high-stakes tests but waste valuable learning opportunities. Stick to the ROLE strategies outlined in this book, and your students will learn more than ever. On top of that, your administrators will be happy when the test results arrive.

ROLEizing Even the Toughest Class

When I first converted my classroom to a Results Only Learning Environment, I had five sections of 7th grade Language Arts. Four classes took to results-only learning very quickly, and my "no rules" and "no consequences" philosophy was an immediate success. The students in those four classes loved the freedom and autonomy the class provided. My fifth class was different. Nearly half the students in this class had learning disabilities, and numerous others were at risk of failure. In fact, most of the 16 students in that class received at least one *F* in another subject during the school year. The problem these kids were facing, decades of experience tell me, is that they have never embraced learning, mainly because traditional methods have conditioned them to hate school. At-risk students are difficult to engage in learning and tend to be disruptive in class. It's rare to have a full schedule of "dream classes" in which every student immediately loves learning and behaves perfectly, and the aforementioned description of at-risk students is a pretty accurate illustration of my one tough class from my first ROLE year.

In prior years, I would have gone to the "my-way-or-the-highway" toolbox and started isolating students or calling parents with complaints and threats. Soon, I would have tried to dissuade them from disrupting class with worksheets and other boring activities. Eventually, I would have sent them to the principal's office. As a ROLE teacher, though, I was determined to engage these previously low-achieving students in ways they hadn't seen. It would have been easy to change my methods the first time a student said, "This is stupid" or "I don't like reading." Instead, I remained steadfast in making results-only strategies habitual for all students. When the student who routinely left his materials in his locker came to class empty-handed on several consecutive days, I allowed him to return to his locker without complaint. "We read every day," I said. "You're missing valuable in-class reading time if you don't bring your book." Soon, heading back to his locker to grab a paperback novel became less important than getting to class on time so he could read and discuss books with his peers, and the tardies dissipated.

Another student was removed by other teachers on a weekly basis for constant disruptions. When she interrupted my minilessons, I ignored her until the individual or group activities began. Then I invited her into the hallway for a sidebar, explaining how difficult it was for me to be successful while she was interrupting. I told her that other students modeled what she did because she possessed leadership qualities. Although this student never became a "star," her behavior improved and the class became more successful.

That class was never easy for me. Several days a week, I was frustrated by students who were disengaged, even when I was delivering the same lesson that other classes loved. The key for me was consistency and determination. On days that I felt a student was getting the best of me, I reminded myself that if I gave in and allowed a student to do nothing or if I punished a student out of anger, I would be failing the results-only system and—more important—I'd be failing the student and his or her peers.

When you have the proverbial "class from hell," remember that those students need you and a ROLE more than the classes filled with students who are not at risk of failure. The key is your commitment to a ROLE. When students see that you believe in autonomy and the elimination of carrots and sticks, they will come around eventually. When they see that it's important to you that they remain in class to learn, rather than being sent to the office at the first sign of disagreement, it won't be long before they value the system. Your reward for getting students to embrace learning is one that is very rare in education. Enjoy it, and become a champion of the system that made it possible.

Get Creative

The summer after my first year of using results-only learning, I wasted little time thinking of new ways to augment my successful ROLE strategies. I wanted to improve the existing year-long projects and continue the complete implementation of project-based learning. My students completed an amazing reading project at the end of the year, integrating a wide variety of Web 2.0 tools to demonstrate what they had learned over the course of an entire school year and through dozens of books. The project had all the parts of a results-only activity, but I still wanted more. I began looking for additional online tools, and I considered ways that students could integrate them into the project. This still wasn't sufficient.

If autonomy was indeed the best part of a ROLE, I thought, I had to give my students even more freedom than I had provided them during the previous year. It wasn't enough to just give them a menu of choices on our projects; instead, I had to get them to *create* the projects. As the school year progressed, I wanted them to take even more control of their own learning, but this takes a lot of creativity. If you're like me, you may not be the most creative teacher in the school. I get most of my creative ideas from a few places. My wife is one source of help, and my Personal Learning Network is another. I follow hundreds of excellent teachers on Twitter and read dozens of fine education blogs. The successful results-only classroom is constantly changing. Since there are no recyclable worksheets and homework assignments, it's important to keep the learning fresh. Online tools and social media reveal new methods daily. The ROLE teacher must stay current on these applications and decide how to use them in a workshop setting and on year-long projects while at the same time teach them to students so they can create their own learning opportunities. With this thirst for creativity in mind, I spend much of the summer learning about new technology tools and how to integrate them into my classroom.

When you convert your classroom to a ROLE, you may want to consider some of these strategies for creativity. If you're not using Twitter, you should be. Follow me, the people I follow, or other teachers, and you'll be on your way to amazing, free professional development. Search for education bloggers, especially those in your subject area and grade. There are thousands of remarkable teachers sharing their own progressive, ROLE-like strategies. Most important, though, always ask yourself what will give your students autonomy and a thirst for learning. How can you make your class a student-centered learning community?

Considering the Possibilities

All positive change in the world comes from our ideas of what we believe is possible.

—*Alexandra Jamieson*

When this book's manuscript was first reviewed by educators, there was plenty of skepticism. It was all too appropriate that I was given feedback about a ROLE, and I wasn't too surprised to see a mix of people who were inspired by such a bold system of education reform along with skeptics who failed to completely grasp its vision. I don't see those educators who are unconvinced about the possible success of a ROLE as stubborn, and I don't immediately label them traditionalists, but I do ask them to be open-minded.

I don't want to suggest that all traditionalists are bad teachers. I work with wonderful people who dedicate their lives to inspiring their students. Many arrive to school early and leave late. I'm sure they believe, as I once did, they are doing everything to help their students. I know many of them, even those who call me friend, are skeptical about results-only learning. Again, I say, please open your mind to the possibilities. For the sake of your students, give results-only learning a chance, even if only for a short time.

For at least one school year, embrace a ROLE. Discard your worksheets and stop assigning homework. Stop giving quizzes and turn your tests into diagnostics to evaluate understanding. Remember, very few students can demonstrate mastery of numerous learning outcomes in a four-week unit of study with one multiple-choice test. Tell your students that you'd like to give them some freedom—that you're more interested in learning than in rules and consequences. Instead of placing a number on their papers and projects, provide meaningful narrative feedback and give them a chance to make changes so they can demonstrate real learning. Allow your students to evaluate their progress and at least take part in deciding their final report card grades.

In a world rife with standards and high-stakes testing, educators are driven to assess. In my school district, many teachers test their students weekly. The kids hate it. I know this because I talk to them about it. One time, during a quarterly evaluation conference, an insightful 14-year-old told me she was visiting private schools and planned to leave our school district the following year. She couldn't read as much as she wanted, she complained, because she spent countless hours preparing for weekly tests and completing rote-memory homework assignments. As much as she hated this, her desire for good grades forced her to abandon independent reading so she could score well and maintain her honors standing. My own children have asked me why they have to take tests every week. Imagine the difficulty this presented as I was forced to justify the broken system in which I work. My children, though, have learned that I will not submit my students to the irrelevant and impractical methods that most traditional teachers use. I have made a commitment to do what I know is best and what truly impacts student learning.

I believe it's time for you and all teachers to consider making a commitment to the kind of change that's been discussed throughout this book. Consider the possibility that for real learning to take place, the barriers must be stripped away. This means assessment, for the most part, has to stop. You can evaluate without assessing. Teachers have to get out of students' way and let them discover their own paths. Let them falter. Let them fall down. Deny the urge to help them up. Know that when you give them less, they will eventually produce more. Trust them. Ask deep, probing questions, and allow your students to spend a whole year finding the answers. Challenge them to ask questions of their own along the way. Consider the value of lengthy collaborative projects over nightly homework, daily worksheets, and multiple-choice assignments. Consider how much students will learn when evaluation consists of conversations about what they produce—conversations that summarize, explain, redirect, and request resubmission of activities so mastery learning can take place.

Resist the urge to say "I can't" or "I don't have time." Remember that my transition from traditional teacher to ROLE teacher happened over a single summer. As Paul Anderson says, "Summer break is great because you get a break from school, but you also can reinvent your class, make it something that it's never been before" (2012). What's the worst thing that can happen if you change and it doesn't work out? Anderson wonders. "If you can drink that bottle [of passion], also remembering to fail, learn, and then repeat the process over again, then I think you'll have a life worth living."

One Last Anecdote

Three-quarters of a school year had passed, and we were heading into spring break. It was one of those laid-back days that end with students assembling in the gymnasium for a dodge ball game supporting a school fundraiser. Classes that day consisted of project work, quiet socializing, and some individual conferences. I was leaving feedback for a student on our class blog when a young lady in the class approached my desk. She was always courteous and typically wore a pleasant smile.

On this day, though, she seemed agitated. "What's up?" I asked, addressing her by name. She paused and slid a withdrawal sheet onto my desk.

"I'm moving," she whispered. "Today's my last day." As I have always done when any student moves away, I frowned and told her that we'd certainly miss her and that she had been a great asset to our class. I signed her form, passed it back, and wished her the best of luck. I glanced back at my computer screen and studied my work for a few seconds before I realized she was still standing there. I paused again and looked up. "Is there something else?" I asked. She glanced nervously at her shoes, reluctant to forge ahead. "What is it?" I urged.

"I'd like to keep working on my MAD project," she whispered, "and I was hoping you could continue to give me feedback somehow."

A wide grin lit up my face, and for a moment, I was afraid tears might well up in my eyes. "Absolutely," I said. "I love that you want to finish it. Just keep placing your work on our website, and I'll leave feedback each time you update it. I can't wait to see how your project turns out." She nodded and curled her lips into that familiar smile, thanked me, and bounced happily back to her seat. I started to return to my typing but stopped momentarily to consider the impact of what had just happened. This young lady was, officially at least, no longer my student, yet she wanted me to continue to evaluate the year-long project she'd started many months ago. Her final report card grade for the quarter was already turned in and her books were returned. She had no further responsibility to me, but she still wanted my feedback.

I mused about the possibility that this student might just represent the future of education. She was the product of a Results Only Learning Environment. For one more moment, I thought that just maybe, someday soon, all teachers would begin considering the possibilities.

References

Allington, R., & Gabriel, R. E. (2012). Every child every day. *Educational Leadership, 69*(6), 10–15.

Anderson, P. (2012). C*lassroom game design: Paul Anderson at TEDxBozeman [Video]. Posted April 2012.* http://www.youtube.com/watch?v=4qlYGX0H6Ec

Atwell, N. (2007). *The reading zone: How to help kids become skilled, passionate, habitual, critical readers.* Scholastic: New York

Barnes, M. (2011). How narrative feedback can crush the ABCs. *ASCD Express, 7*(3), Retrieved from http://www.ascd.org/ascd-express/vol7/703-barnes.aspx

Black, P., Harrison, C., Lee, C., Marshall, B., & Wiliam, D. (2004). Working inside the black box: Assessment for learning in the classroom. *Phi Delta Kappan, 86*(1), 9–21.

Bloomfield, D. (2011, June 26). Research calls data-driven education reform into question. *Huffington Post Education.* Retrieved from http://www.huffingtonpost.com/david-bloomfield/education-reform-standardized-testing_b_882718.html

Bower, J. (2011, May 11). My de-grading philosophy Q & A [blog post]. Retrieved from *for the love of learning* at http://www.joebower.org/2011/05/my-grading-philosophy-q.html

Copeland, M. (2005). *Socratic circles: Fostering critical and creative thinking in middle and high school.* Portland: Stenhouse.

Dean, C. B., Hubbell, E. R., Pitler, H., & Stone, B. (2012). *Classroom instruction that works: Research-based strategies for increasing student achievement* (2nd ed.). Denver: McREL.

Earl, R. (2012, May 18). Do cell phones belong in the classroom? *The Atlantic*. Retrieved from http://www.theatlantic.com/national/archive/2012/05/do-cell-phones-belong-in-the-classroom/257325/

Forget, M. A. (2004). *Max teaching with reading and writing: classroom activities for helping students learn new subject matter while acquiring literacy skills*. Portsmouth, VA: Trafford.

Guskey, T. (2011). Five obstacles to grading reform. *Educational Leadership, 69*(3), 16–21.

Hattie J., & Timperly H. (2007). The power of feedback. *Review of Educational Research, 77*(1), 81–112.

Himmele, P., & Himmele, W. (2011). *Total participation techniques: Making every student an active learner*. Alexandria, VA: ASCD.

Jenkins, N. (2011). Shut up and teach [Presentation]. Retrieved from http://prezi.com/j_wkwyalz-lx/shut-up-and-teach/

Kohn, A. (2000). *The schools our children deserve: Moving beyond traditional classrooms and "tough standards."* New York: Houghton Mifflin.

Kohn, A. (2006a). *Beyond discipline: From compliance to community*. Alexandria, VA: ASCD.

Kohn, A. (2006b). *The homework myth: Why our kids get too much of a bad thing*. Philadelphia: Da Capo Press.

Kohn, A. (2011). The case against grades. *Educational Leadership, 69*(3), 28–33.

Krashen, S. (2011a). Our schools are not broken: The problem is poverty. Commencement speech given at the Graduate School of Education & Counseling, Lewis and Clark College, Portland, OR, June 2011.

Krashen, S. (2011b). Protecting students against the effects of poverty: Libraries. *New England Reading Association Journal, 46*(2), 17–21, 102.

Kuntz, B. (2011). Build personal relationships to boost students' self-esteem. *Education Update, 53*(12), 8.

Kuntz, B. (2012). Focus on learning, not grades. *Education Update, 54*(5), 3.

Larmer, J. (2011, July 1). Debunking five myths about project-based learning [blog post]. Retrieved from *Edutopia* at http://www.edutopia.org/blog/debunking-five-pbl-myths-john-larmer

Lenhart, A. (2012, March 19). Teens, smartphones & texting [blog post]. Retrieved from *Pew Internet* at http://pewinternet.org/Reports/2012/Teens-and-smartphones/Cell-phone-ownership/Smartphones.aspx

Maiers, A., & Sandvold, A. (2011) *The passion driven classroom: A framework for teaching & learning*. Larchmont, NY: Eye On Education.

Markham, T. (2011, June 21). Want better project-based learning? Use social and emotional learning [blog post]. Retrieved from *Edutopia* at http://www.edutopia.org/blog/project-based-learning-social-emotional-learning-thom-markham

Marzano, R. J., & Marzano, J. S. (2003). The key to classroom management. *Educational Leadership, 61*(1), 6–13.

Miller, D. (2009). *The book whisperer: Awakening the inner reader in every child.* San Francisco: Jossey-Bass.

Montalvo, G. P., Mansfield, E. A., & Miller, R. B. (2007). Liking or disliking the teacher: Student motivation, engagement and achievement. *Evaluation and Research in Education, 20*(3), 144–158.

National Governors Association Center for Best Practices, Council of Chief State School Officers. (2010). Common Core State Standards.

NewWOW. (2011, June 9). NetWORK News 6/9/11 [blog post]. Retrieved from *NewWOW* at http://www.newwow.net/network-news-6911

Nielsen, L. (2012, May 9). Why BYOD, not banning cell phones, is the answer [blog post]. Retrieved from *THE Journal* at http://thejournal.com/articles/2012/05/09/why-byod-not-banning-cell-phones-is-the-answer.aspx

Perkins, D. (2008). *Making learning whole: How seven principles of teaching can transform education.* San Francisco: Jossey-Bass.

Peters, T. (2003). *Re-Imagine: Business excellence in a disruptive age.* London: Dorling Kindersley Limited.

Pink, D. (2009). *Drive: The surprising truth about what motivates us.* New York: Riverhead Books.

Quaglia, R. J., & Fox, K. M. (2003). *Student aspirations: Eight conditions that make a difference.* Champaign, IL: Research Press.

Ressler, C., & Thompson, J. (2008). *Why work sucks and how to fix it: No schedules, no meetings, no joke—The simple change that can make your job terrific.* New York: Penguin.

Ripp, P. (2011a, June 15). So I gave up punishment and the kids still behaved [blog post]. Retrieved from *Blogging through the Fourth Dimension* at http://www.pernilleripp.com/2011/06/so-i-gave-up-punishment-and-kids-still.html

Ripp, P. (2011b, November 20). 10 ways to make it "their" room [blog post]. Retrieved from *Blogging through the Fourth Dimension* at http://www.pernilleripp.com/2011/11/10-ways-to-make-it-their-room.html

RSA Animate. (2010, April 1). RSA Animate—Drive: The surprising truth about what motivates us [Video]. Posted April 2010. http://www.youtube.com/watch?v=u6XAPnuFjJc

Schaps, E. (2003). Creating a school community. *Educational Leadership, 60*(6), 31–33.

Stansbury, M. (2011, July 7). Los Angeles schools declare: enough with homework [blog post]. Retrieved from *eSchool News* at http://www.eschoolnews.com/2011/07/07/los-angeles-schools-declare-enough-with-homework

Stevenson, A. (2011, June 10). Just shut up and listen, expert tells teachers [blog post]. Retrieved from *The Sydney Morning Herald* at http://www.smh.com.au/national/education/just-shut-up-and-listen-expert-tells-teachers-20110609-1fv9y.html

Sullo, B. (2009). *The motivated student: Unlocking the enthusiasm for learning.* Alexandria, VA: ASCD.

Vail, J. (2011, October 11). Feedback and mastery learning [blog post]. Retrieved from *ROLE Reversal* at http://resultsonlylearning.blogspot.com/2011/10/feedback-and-mastery-learning.html

Volante, L. (2004). Teaching to the test: What every educator and policymaker should know. *Canadian Journal of Educational Administration and Policy, 35.* Retrieved from http://www.umanitoba.ca/publications/cjeap/articles/volante.html

Wiliam, D. (2011). *Embedded formative assessment.* Bloomington, IN: Solution Tree.

Winne, P. H., & Butler, D. L. (1994). Student cognition in learning from teaching. In T. Husen & T. Postlewaite (Eds.), *International encyclopaedia of education* (2nd ed., pp 5738–5745). Oxford, UK: Pergamon.

Index

The letter *f* following a page number denotes a figure.

About the Author

Mark Barnes is a 20-year classroom teacher and creator of the Results Only Learning Environment (ROLE), a progressive, student-centered classroom that eliminates all traditional teaching methods, including grades. While transforming his classroom into a ROLE, Mark has also revolutionized K–12 web-based instruction by bringing private student websites into his classroom—an extension of school into cyberspace. Mark has developed five online courses on digital strategies for educators, taught through two accredited colleges in Ohio. A popular speaker and presenter, Mark is also a Discovery Education Network Star Educator, honored for his work in education technology. Mark is the creator of the website Learnitin5.com, a library of videos that demonstrate how to use virtually any Web 2.0 and social media application in the classroom. Mark's classroom website, www.barnesclass.com, was recognized in 2011 by Indiana University's School of Education as one of the top 10 K–12 classroom websites in the United States. Mark resides in a suburb of Cleveland, Ohio, with his wife and two children.

Readers can follow Mark Barnes on Twitter at @markbarnes19. He can also be reached via e-mail at mark@thepaperlessclassroom.com. In addition to creating videos at Learnitin5.com, Mark blogs regularly at resultsonlylearning.com and ascdedge.ascd.org.

Related ASCD Resources

At the time of publication, the following ASCD resources were available (ASCD stock numbers appear in parentheses). For up-to-date information about ASCD resources, go to www.ascd.org. You can search the complete archives of *Educational Leadership* at http://www.ascd.org/el.

ASCD Edge

Exchange ideas and connect with other educators on the social networking site ASCD Edge™ at http://ascdedge.ascd.org/

Print Products

Advancing Formative Assessment in Every Classroom: A Guide for Instructional Leaders by Connie M. Moss and Susan M. Brookhart (#109031)

Assignments Matter: Making the Connections That Help Students Meet Standards by Eleanor Dougherty (#112048)

Breaking Free from Myths About Teaching and Learning: Innovation as an Engine for Student Success by Allison Zmuda (#109041)

Checking for Understanding: Formative Assessment Techniques for Your Classroom by Douglas Fisher and Nancy Frey (#107023)

The Classroom of Choice: Giving Students What They Need and Getting What You Want by Jonathan C. Erwin (#104020)

Inspiring the Best in Students by Jonathan C. Erwin (#110006)

Productive Group Work: How to Engage Students, Build Teamwork, and Promote Understanding by Nancy Frey, Douglas Fisher, and Sandi Everlove (#109018)

Rethinking Homework: Best Practices That Support Diverse Needs by Cathy Vatterott (#108071)

Total Participation Techniques: Making Every Student an Active Learner by Pérsida Himmele and William Himmele (#111037)

Transformative Assessment by W. James Popham (#108018)

What Teachers Really Need to Know About Formative Assessment by Laura Greenstein (#110017)

THE WHOLE CHILD The Whole Child Initiative helps schools and communities create learning environments that allow students to be healthy, safe, engaged, supported, and challenged. To learn more about other books and resources that relate to the whole child, visit www.wholechildeducation.org.

For more information: send e-mail to member@ascd.org; call 1-800-933-2723 or 703-578-9600, press 2; send a fax to 703-575-5400; or write to Information Services, ASCD, 1703 N. Beauregard St., Alexandria, VA 22311-1714 USA.